Allen O Myers, Allen Myers

Bosses and boodle in Ohio politics

Some plain truths for honest people

Allen O Myers, Allen Myers

Bosses and boodle in Ohio politics
Some plain truths for honest people

ISBN/EAN: 9783337134020

Printed in Europe, USA, Canada, Australia, Japan

Cover: Foto ©Suzi / pixelio.de

More available books at **www.hansebooks.com**

BOSSES and BOODLE

IN

OHIO POLITICS.

Some Plain Truths for Honest People.

HON. ALLEN O. MYERS.
(*Pickaway.*)

1895.
CINCINNATI, OHIO:
LYCEUM PUBLISHING CO.,
P. O. BOX 23.

DEDICATION.

That it may be known to all who choose to read, that the flight
of time has not destroyed a deep sense of gratitude to those
who were gracious to a life when beset by darkness,
and who were friends, when friends were few,
this work, written for the good of the people,
and as a protest against a great and
growing crime, is dedicated to

HON. O. E. NILES, DR. SAM'L TURNEY,

AND

HON. GEO. W. GREGG,

CITIZENS OF MY NATIVE TOWN,
CIRCLEVILLE, O.

BOSSES

and

BOODLE.

"The control of elections and legislation, by the corrupt use of money, more than anything else, menaces popular government and the public peace! If these abuses are not speedily checked, the consequences are likely to be disastrous!"

JUDGE WALTER Q. GRESHAM.

PREFACE.

THE preacher has said that "To everything there is a season, and a time to every purpose under the heavens; a time to keep silence and a time to speak!" This is an opportune time to speak plainly and boldly upon the question of "Bosses and Boodle" in Ohio politics. Twice within ten years the people of Ohio have seen their representatives freely purchased; the Legislature has been brazenly debauched; the people have been betrayed for a price; law and decency have been shamelessly violated and wickedly outraged; seats in the United States Senate have been knocked down to the highest bidder, and through the unlawful, profuse, and corrupt use of money, Henry B. Payne, of Cleveland, Ohio, and Calvin S. Brice, of Wall Street, New York City, have secured honors (?) to which they were not entitled. In the case of Henry B. Payne a plea in abatement may be entered. He was not a party to the purchase, but the evils resulting from the debasement of the sworn representatives of a free people were equally as great and appalling.

In the case of Calvin S. Brice there are no mitigating circumstances. His agents proceeded, under his personal direction, to the most deliberate defiance of the will of a free people, and the most audacious, bold and devilish methods human ingenuity ever devised to acquire an office without the honor. These acts as consummated are plague spots of infamy upon the tarnished name of a great commonwealth. It is the purpose of this work to give some of the details of these crimes, hoping thereby to arouse the people of Ohio, and make their repetition dangerous to the perpetrators and participants, if not impossible.

ALLEN O. MYERS.

No. 22 Morris St., Cincinnati, O.

TABLE OF CONTENTS.

THE LION IN THE PATH OF THE BOODLERS.

(*From Cincinnati Porcupine, 1889.*)

BOSSES AND BOODLE.

CHAPTER I.

INTRODUCTORY.

THIS IS BOODLE'S GOD.

"THE past thirty years has witnessed the enormous increase of individual and corporate fortunes in this country, until the millionaire is no longer a rarity! This fact has served to develop the insolence and arrogance of wealth, until intellectual endowments are dwarfed in its sordid pretense, and moral character lies prostrate in its ruthless path! [Applause.] The power to rule men by intellectual and moral forces, the test of a statesmanship of a former day, is fast passing away. While wealth, the uncrowned king, oftentimes lacking both, and coveting neither, arrogantly seeks to rule in a domain where it is scarcely fitted to sway; its altar has been erected in every community, and its votaries are found in every household. Patriotism has given place to material expediency, and the love of country is supplanted by the love of money. An aptness for percentages and the successful manipulation of railroads and stock boards are often regarded as the most essential of senatorial equipments."—*Speech of Hon. Henry St. George Tucker, in the National House of Representatives, July 12, 1892.*

I. In the last few years, the judge upon the bench; the patriot in the halls of legislation; the fearless and intelligent preacher, and a courageous and incorruptible press, (the truest exponent of public opinion,) have lifted their united voices in warning a slow and slothful people against the great and growing evils of bribery and corruption, which pervade the official life of our government, defeat the ends and purposes of our free institutions and menace their very existence.

II. Ohio became a state March 1, 1803. The first legislature, which convened at Chillicothe, O., on this day, carried into effect the provisions of the new constitution adopted in November, 1802, by canvassing the vote cast for state officers, at an election held Jan. 11, 1803, and Edward Tiffin was declared elected Governor and was at once inaugurated, succeeding the territorial government headed by Gov. Arthur St. Clair. Thomas Worthington, of Ross, and John Smith, of Hamilton, were elected to represent the state in the United States Senate.

III. The list below gives the names of those who have been elected to serve, or appointed to fill vacancies as Senators from Ohio, since the foundation of the state, with the Congresses in which each served and the years of service:

Thomas Worthington, Ross County, 8th, 9th, 11th to 13th Congress; 1803—1811; 1813—1815.

John Smith, Hamilton County, 8th to 10th Congress; 1803—1809.

Edward Tiffin, Ross County, 10th to 11th Congress; 1809—1811.

Return J. Meigs, Washington County, 10th to 11th Congress; 1809—1811.

Alexander Campbell, Brown County, 11th to 12th Congress; 1811—1813.

Stanley Griswold, Cuyahoga County, 11th Congress; 1809—1811.

Jeremiah Morrow, Warren County, 13th to 15th Congress; 1383—1817.

Joseph Kerr, Ross County, 13th Congress: 1813—1815.

Benjamin Ruggles, Belmont Co., 14th to 22d Congress; 1815—1833.

Wm. A. Trimble, Highland Co., 16th, 17th Congress; 1819—1823.

Ethan A. Brown, Hamilton Co., 17th, 18th Congress; 1821—1825.

William H. Harrison, Hamilton County, 19th, 20th Congress; 1825—1829.

Jacob Burnet, Hamilton County, 20th, 21st Congress; 1827—1831.

Thos. Ewing, Fairfield County, 22d, 24th to 31st Congress; 1831—1833; 1835—1849.

Thomas Morris, Clermont County, 23d to 25th Congress; 1833—1839.

William Allen, Ross County, 25th to 30th Congress; 1837—1849.

Benjamin Tappan, Jefferson County, 26th to 28th Congress; 1839—1841.

Thomas Corwin, Warren County, 29th to 31st Congress; 1845—1851.

Salmon P. Chase, Hamilton County, 31st to 33d, 37th Congress; 1849—1855; 1861—1863.

Benjamin F. Wade, Ashtabula County, 32d to 40th Congress; 1851—1869.

George E. Pugh, Hamilton County, 34th to 36th Congress; 1855—1861.

John Sherman, Richland County, 37th to 45th, 47th to 54th Congress; 1861—1875; 1881—1899.

Allen G. Thurman, Franklin County, 41st to 46th Congress; 1869—1881.

Stanley Matthews, Hamilton County, 45th Congress; 1877—1879.

George H. Pendleton, Hamilton County, 46th to 48th Congress; 1879—1885.

Henry B. Payne, Cuyahoga County, 49th, 50th Congress; 1885—1889.

Calvin S. Brice, of New York, 51st, 53d, 54th Congress; 1891—1897.

In 1809 John Smith resigned and Return J. Meigs, Jr., was chosen to serve during the unexpired term; and he resigned in 1810 to accept the office of Governor of Ohio. In 1814 Thomas Worthington resigned to accept the office of Governor of Ohio, and Joseph

Kerr, of Ross, was chosen to serve the unexpired term. In 1822, Wm. A. Trimble, of Highland, died during his term of office, from wounds received at Ft. Erie, in 1812, and Ethan A. Brown, of Hamilton, was chosen to serve the unexpired term. In 1828, Wm. Henry Harrison, afterwards President, resigned his office as Senator, to accept an appointment as Minister to Colombia, and Judge Jacob Burnet, of Hamilton, was selected to fill the vacancy. In 1861 Salmon P. Chase resigned his seat in the Senate to accept a place in President Lincoln's Cabinet, and John Sherman, of Richland, was chosen to fill the vacancy. In 1877 John Sherman resigned to accept a place in President Hayes' Cabinet, and Stanley Matthews, of Hamilton, was chosen to serve the unexpired term, and was afterwards made Chief Justice. In 1880, James A. Garfield was chosen United States Senator, but the same year he was elected President of the United States and resigned the Senatorship in in January, 1881; and John Sherman left the office of Secretary of the Treasury to resume his seat in the Senate. The old saying: "that few die and none resign," is amply proven by the Senators from Ohio. Only one has died while holding the office; six have resigned, and five of these did so to accept other offices.

IV. The questions that concerned the people of Ohio for the first half century of the state's existence, were those that related chiefly to a young and growing state, such as the payment for public lands; the war of 1812; the banks and currency; public schools; internal improvements, and the question of slavery, which was always a living, burning issue, until settled by the appeal to arms. The constitution of 1802 was a weak and unsatisfactory instrument, and one unworthy of a state born under the broad and beneficent principles of the ordinance of 1787. But the arbitrary and military methods of that old, blundering and ever unfortunate soldier, Arthur St. Clair, had provoked the opposition and aroused the strongest passions and prejudices of the early settlers and hardy pioneers who had sought the wilderness to find freedom and homes for themselves and their families. Their love of liberty, the spirit of the age and their surroundings caused them to oppose the methods and acts of the semi-military territorial government, and hastened the steps necessary to the formation of a new state government. When empowered by an act of Congress to select representatives to frame a constitution in 1802, the nine counties comprising the territory now known as Ohio, sent as representatives to the constitutional convention, men who were bitterly opposed to the territorial Governor, his policy and acts. They proceeded to frame a constitution, and in thirty days completed a plan of government which provided an executive head without a prerogative. The existence of Gov. Arthur St. Clair was a menace that constantly overawed and made afraid.

There was no thought of the future. They did not seem to realize that they were laying the foundations of a state that would soon rise and stand as a master-miracle in an age of miracles. The powers and patronage that should have been vested in the chief executive, were left in the hands of the legislative department, when, as it proved, the abuses and demoralizing influences of patronage were unlimited, without any compensating results, and with no person or officer to hold responsible for the abuse of power and the misuse of patronage. On this subject, Hon. Rufus King, in his very excellent history of "the Commonwealth of Ohio," has this to say:

"The instrument so adopted, it would be respectful to pass in silence. It was framed by men of little experience in matters of state, and under circumstances unfavorable to much forecast. With such a model of simplicity and strength before them as the national constitution, which had just been formed, the wonder is that some of its ideas were not borrowed.

"It seems to have been studiously disregarded; and Ohio, as well as some states further westward, which her emigrant sons with filial regard induced to adopt her example, has suffered ever since from a weak form of government, made up in haste and apparently in mortal dread of Governor St. Clair. He declined to be a candidate for the office of Governor, but unluckily not until the convention had adjourned. In after years, Ohio's greatest and wittiest Governor* was wont to say, that, after passing the first week of

---

Tom Corwin.

his administration with nothing to do, he had taken an inquest of the office, and found that reprieving criminals and appointing notaries were the sole 'flowers of the prerogative.'

"Briefly stated, it was a government which had no executive; a half starved, short-lived judiciary, and a lop-sided legislature. This department, overloaded with the appointing power which had been taken away from the executive, became so much depraved in the traffic of offices, that, in an assembly* where there was a tie vote between the Democrats and the Whigs, two 'Free Soilers' held the balance of power, and were permitted to choose a United States Senator in consideration of giving their votes for every other appointment to the party which aided them in this supreme exploit of jobbery. A new constitution put an end to this, but the shadow of St. Clair still predominates."

V. Up to the election of Salmon P. Chase to the United States Senate, in 1848, by the methods charged by Rufus King, by which the patronage at the disposal of the legislature was bartered for two votes for United States Senator, there had been no attempt made and no act charged of a character to corrupt the members of the legislature and defeat the will of the people in the choice of a United States Senator. Even the election of Salmon P. Chase by the methods charged, was not a miscarriage or a defeat of the will of the people, as a few years later, in 1857, in the contest for Governor of Ohio, he defeated

* The legislature of 1848.

Henry B. Payne in a close and exciting contest. The Constitution of Ohio, adopted in 1851, remedied many of the defects of the state government, and a very radical and commendable change was made in removing the appointing power from the legislature, but the use of Federal patronage by United States officials had become an evil so great as to call forth the severest condemnation from those who were apprehensive for public weal, and desirous of preserving the purity of our political institutions. In 1835, during President Jackson's second term, a committee of the Senate, of which Jno. C. Calhoun was chairman, was appointed to investigate the question of "executive patronage," and in a report the following language was used: "It is easy to see that the certain, direct and inevitable tendency of this practice is to convert the entire body of those in office into corrupt and supple instruments of power, and to raise up a host of hungry, greedy and subservient partisans, ready for every service, however base and corrupt. Were a premium offered for the best means of extending to the utmost the power of patronage; to destroy the love of country and substitute a spirit of subserviency and man-worship; to encourage vice and discourage virtue, and, in a word, to prepare for the subversion of liberty and the establishment of despotism, no scheme more perfect could be devised." As years passed laws were created to restrict the disposal of patronage in the gift of the chief executive of our composite system of government; and to placate the persistent opposition of the Senate, the President, in a measure, ceded to the Senators the control and disposition of the offices in the states. The Civil War of 1861–5 seemed to suspend constitution and law, and change the purpose and genius of our institutions. The vast expenditures necessary to maintain our armies and carry on the war, were met by extraordinary taxation on domestic and foreign industries. This necessitated a ten-fold increase in the number of government officials. A paper money, the issue of bonds, the creation of a highly favored system of banking, gave a tremendous impulse to all commercial and industrial energies. Quick-witted men and keen-eyed capital were swift to take advantage of the opportunities presented under the unnatural and changed conditions brought about by the War of the Rebellion. Vulgar men grew rich, public and private morals decayed, monopolies flourished, syndicates and combinations were born and thrived in the hour of the nation's peril, and the god that Washington Irving styled the Almighty Dollar, became the chief deity, enshrined in the temple of liberty and worshiped by the American people.

VI. It is not until recent years that we have begun to reap the legitimate fruits of the demoralizing conditions and legislation that grew up during and out of the war. But it is doubtful if, up to 1884, any man chosen to the United States Senate from Ohio, owed his election to either patronage or money. There is no doubt but that both had been used to influence and control members of the legislature, but only in a few cases. No open charges against any one had been made in the press. But these practices began to lift their brazen heads, from year to year, after the war, until it became necessary to enact laws to restrain them. The existence of such laws, is an evidence of the presence, in the body politic, of the evils of corruption, that needed the wholesome and restraining check of the law. The following is the law of Ohio upon the subject of bribery, which is classified under the head of "Offenses against Public Justice."

SEC. 6900. Whoever corruptly gives, promises, or offers to any member or officer of the general assembly, or of either house thereof, or to any state judicial, or other officer, or any public trustee, or any agent or employe of the state, or of such officer or trustee, either before or after his election, qualification, appointment, or employment, any valuable thing; or corruptly offers or promises to do any act beneficial to any such person, to influence him with respect to his official duty, or to influence his action, vote, opinion, or judgment, in any matter pending or that might legally come before him, and whoever, being a member of the legislature, or a state, or other officer, or public trustee, or agent or trustee, employe of the state or of such officer, or trustee, either before or after his election, qualification, appointment, or employment, solicits or accepts any such valuable or beneficial thing to influence him with respect to his official duty, or to influence his action, vote, opinion, or judgment in any matter pending or that might legally come before him, shall be imprisoned in the penitentiary not more than five years, or fined not more than five hundred dollars, or both. A person convicted under this section, is disqualified from holding any public office or appointment under this state; and if not a state officer, shall be removed from office or employment by order of the court.

This section is a consolidation of laws that were passed at three different periods, 1830, 1860 and 1870. With a single exception no one has ever been convicted under this act, and no officer has ever been indicted, and charged with accepting bribe by a Court of Justice, although public opinion has laid this crime against public justice at the doors of many. A few years ago, a lobbyist named Watson, was tried and convicted at Columbus, O., for offering a bribe to a member of the legislature. Watson's real offense was in not really giving to the virtuous legislator what he had recklessly offered or promised. He was found guilty because he did not do business on a cash basis. A close examination of the law of Ohio, to prevent bribery, will show, that there is really no law to punish a member of the legislature who receives money to vote for any person for United States Senator. The law does not apply to the caucus system that is in vogue and which governs our politics. It is not an offense under the law for a man to sell his vote in caucus. Of course no member of the legislature has ever said, or would ever think of taking money in office or anything that would in any way influence his vote in violation of the plain provisions of the law.

VII. The laws of Ohio cover 3,000 pages; most of them relate to the transaction of business, the rights of property and designate the crimes against the same, and the pains and penalties for such offenses. When Moses descended from the awful mountain of Sinai, that flamed, and smoked, and thundered, he brought with him the ten commandments, written with the finger of the living God, on stone tables. The first four of these related to man's duty to his Creator, and the next five fix the duties of man to his family and his fellow man, and forbid certain offenses, and the last and longest is an enactment to prevent the desire to acquire anything of value that is the property of another. In their recent flight from Egypt, the Hebrews had despoiled their masters of all they could carry, which was not much, and in the suffering that beset this people, in their wanderings, the many who had little or nothing were liable to want and take what the few had. In their condition of poverty, there were no offices to sell, and nothing to buy them with, and hence there was no necessity for a law against boodle and boodlers, the greatest of crimes in a popular government.

When Solon, the law-giver, was devising a form of

government and a code of laws for Athens, he called to his assistance as counselors, the wise men and philosophers of surrounding cities. Among these was Anachorsis, a Scythian prince, famous for temperance, justice and knowledge, who ranked as one of the seven wise men of his age. He was a guest in Solon's house, and when he learned of some of the measures Solon proposed, he laughed at the absurdity of Solon in imagining that the avarice and injustice of the Athenians could be restrained by written laws, which in all respects resembled spider's webs, and would, like them, only hold and entangle the poor and weak, while the rich and powerful easily broke them. The history of Athens shows, that the observations of the Scythian were based on an ample knowledge of the inherent vices and weaknesses of mankind.

Every government that has been of enough importance to earn a tombstone in the graveyard of the past; every civilization that has flamed on the horizon of time, like a bright exhalation, with every promise of being permanent, and has gone out in eternal darkness, leaves the same epitaph and the same lamentation of failure. No race of men have yet proven strong enough to resist the corrupt influences of wealth. The wit of man, guided by the disasters that stand like mile posts along the progress of the race, has not been able to devise a code of laws to restrain their own cupidity and to protect society from the debauching influences of corrupt and designing men of great wealth, who are determined to purchase honors and place, that their talents, occupations and character prevent them from earning and unfit them to hold. We brand the thief as a criminal; imprison him and clothe him in stripes as an enemy to society and property; but we make social saints out of our millionaires, who purchase seats in the United States Senate, and ostracize all who dare question their title to the purchase.

CHAPTER II.

THE UNITED STATES SENATE.

To hold a place
In a council which was once esteemed an honor
And a reward for virtue, hath quite lost
Lustre and reputation, and is made
A mercenary purchase.

Massinger's Bondman.

There is an old print that represents an historic scene, which marks the birth of American Institutions. A number of stately gentlemen of sombre mien, in black silk stockings and powdered queue, have stood up to have their pictures taken before signing the Declaration of Independence. Each looks as though he had put on his funeral clothes before signing his own death warrant.

II. When the representatives of the colonies found war confronting them, they met to provide methods and means to oppose the power of the mighty empire of Great Britain. There was no turning aside or looking back. It was success or death. Having made up their minds to sacrifice all but honor, and being willing to "give their lives, their fortunes and their sacred honors" to a cause they believed just, they broke forth into that psalm of freedom, the Declaration of Independence. The chords in this hymn of Liberty, represent the divine expression of the aspirations of the human heart, from the birth of governments and oppression. As a national poem, it has no equal; as a song it will soothe the downtrodden and oppressed, through the ages, until other wants and needs of the human heart shall call forth a new and a better one. But while the Declaration of Independence served as a battle-hymn to win our freedom; when the Revolution was over, its mission was ended. The men who drafted it, met in 1787, to frame a form of government for the new-born nation. A constitution was drafted, but not on the principles laid down in the Declaration of Independence. They who had declared "that all men were created free and equal," on the eve of an uncertain war, found other difficulties that beset an impoverished people, and proceeded to legislate for the selfish interests of the colonies. They found their men, black men and red men and white men, and they proceeded to legislate for each. In vain they looked along the shore of time, and scanned the wrecks of governments and civilizations for a model upon which to build their New Ship of State. They found none. They builded, armed and erected a government, of a composite character, unlike any that had ever existed before. When Daniel Webster was proclaiming in stately sentences, the wisdom of our fathers in framing the constitution, the wisest measure that the wisdom of man had ever devised, slaves were selling in the open market at $1200 per head in mixed lots. Wendell Phillips was denouncing his Senator, as a clown and a coward, and branding the federal constitution as a compromise and a crime. It was not until the people and the constitution were baptized in the blood of a civil war, that the instrument was purged of its blots and our boasted free institutions in a measure ceased to be a repudiation of the principles of the Declaration of Independence. On July 4, 1776, our fathers declared that "government derives its just power from the consent of the governed," and eleven years afterward they proceeded to adopt a constitution, in which the people are directly deprived of all voice, in the selection of their servants in three branches of the Federal Government. The people have no voice in the choice of a President, of judicial officers, who are appointed for life, or in the selection of United States Senators.

III. The people—the masses—seemed to be a vulgar herd, unworthy of being trusted, and incapable of understanding their rights and duties in the government about to be created. The checks, so called, upon the people and to restrain the excesses of the mob, constitute the weaknesses of our constitution and our form of government. The great and ever present danger that threatens American institutions to-day, and will menace and destroy if not thwarted by wise changes, is the uncurbed power and excesses of wealth in a thousand forms. Every popular government that has ever lived and perished, has been destroyed by the corrupt and pernicious influences of enormous wealth. While the founders of our government were ever on the alert to check the excesses of the mob, they seemed to overlook what experience has too painfully and repeatedly taught, that property—money, in the hands of dishonest and designing men, are the greatest dangers to fear. Already the dollar mark is over us all. Money is the end of our existence. It is the God we worship. Our government is far from being a representative one. It is ruled by money. Our honors are for sale to the highest bidder. Not at public auction, which would have the merit of increasing prices by open competition, but by private sale. The people are not for sale. The people do not sell, but they are sold. The people are busy. Too busy to give their time and attention to public affairs. But in all communities, and in all sections, there is about one person in one hundred, who is willing to give his time, his talent, and his labors, for the offices and for the money, and thus save the people a great deal of time, labor and money. It is this condition of affairs that makes Bosses a possibility and Boodle a dominant power in our politics. When the people are aroused, as they will be by some dire calamity or some great and open scandal, the constitution and laws will be changed, and "Bosses and Boodle," as the governing and controlling power in our political system will pass away.

IV. In the face of present conditions, it is interesting and instructive to study the proceedings of the constitutional convention, and note the conflicting views and interests, through which the measure had to run before a conclusion was reached, that gave us the body known as the United States Senate. Two sets of opposing views were developed and contended for the mastery in the convention. One party, headed by Alexander Hamilton, favored a strong monarchical government, in all the term implies; and the other party favored a national government, with delegated and restricted bounds, strong enough to protect commerce and trade, and assert its national authority and character, at home and abroad, but reserving all other powers to the states and the people. The creation of the Senate was the most difficult problem the convention had to deal with, and the result, as in other cases, was a compromise of the most dangerous and doubtful character. Prof. J. W. Andrews, in his work on the constitution, quotes the section relating to the Senate and comments as follows:

SEC. 3, *Clause 1.*—The Senate of the United States shall be composed of two Senators from each state, chosen by the legislature thereof for six years, and each Senator shall have one vote.

"In the convention that framed the constitution there was a great difference of opinion as to the mode of electing Senators, as to their term of service, and as to the rule of suffrage. Some were in favor of a nomination by the state legislatures, and an election by the United States House of Representatives, others would have the President appoint from those nominated by the state legislatures; others would have them chosen by the House of Representatives; and others still proposed an election by the people.

"As to the term of office, some advocated a life tenure, or during good behavior; some, a term of nine years; others, seven; others, six; and others, four.

"The question of voting was the most difficult, as in the Continental Congress, the states were on an equality as to their votes, the smaller states wished the same rule to hold under the Constitution, while the larger states claimed that an equality of votes in either House would be unjust. The smaller states finally conceded that in the House of Representatives the number of members should be in proportion to population; but they insisted that in the Senate the states should be equal. But the larger states were tenacious as to the Senate as well as the House, and the committee of the whole reported, 'That the right of suffrage in the second branch of the national legislature ought to be according to the rule established for the first.' This report was adopted by the convention, but the matter was subsequently referred to a committee of one from each state, which reported the rule as it now stands. The final vote was: "Affirmative—Connecticut, New Jersey, Delaware, Maryland, North Carolina—5. Negative—Virginia, Pennsylvania, South Carolina, Georgia—4. Massachusetts, divided." So that this greatest and most difficult of all the important questions which the convention was called upon to solve, was carried by less than a majority of the states represented, and by the concurrence of less than one-third of the represented population.

"Mr. Madison strongly opposed the principle finally adopted. In his letter to Mr. Sparks he said, the Gordian knot of the convention was the question between the larger and smaller states as to the rule of voting in the Senate; the latter claiming, the former opposing the rule of equality.

"By the articles of confederation, each state might send not more than seven delegates to Congress, nor less than two. They were elected annually, but no one could sit more than three years in six. The states could recall their delegates at any time. Under the constitution we see that each state can send two Senators, and as many Representatives as her population entitles her to; that there is nothing to prevent a Senator or Representative from being returned as often as his constituents desire; and that when a Senator or Representative has been elected, the state has no power to recall him.

"Though all the states have the same number of Senators, and each Senator has one vote, that is not the same as voting by states, as was done in the Continental Congress. If both the Senators of a state are present, and vote on opposite sides of a question, their votes neutralize each other, as under the confederation. But if only one of two delegates from a state was present, in the Continental Congress, his vote could not be counted; under the present constitution the vote of a Senator is counted whether his colleague is present or not.

"The constitution does not prescribe the precise method in which the legislature of a state shall choose the Senators, whether by the house voting in joint assembly, or by voting separately. It is not properly an act of legislation, and the governor of a state has no participation in it, as in some states he has in ordinary legislation.

"In 1866 Congress passed an 'Act to regulate the times and manner of holding elections for Senators in Congress.' It provides that the legislature of each state which shall be chosen next preceding the expiration of the time for which any Senator was elected, shall, on the second Tuesday after the meeting and organization thereof, proceed to elect a Senator as follows:

"Each house shall name (propose by vote) a person for Senator by a *viva voce* vote. The next day at noon the two houses shall meet in joint assembly, and if the same person shall have received a majority of all the votes in each house, he shall be declared duly elected.

"If no person has received such majorities, the joint assembly shall choose by a *viva voce* vote; and whoever shall receive a majority of all the votes cast, a majority of each house being present, shall be declared elected.

"If no person is elected the first day, the joint assembly shall convene each day, at twelve o'clock, and take at least one vote each day during the session, or until a Senator is elected.

"If a vacancy exists when the legislature convenes, the same steps shall be taken; and if a vacancy occurs during the session of the legislature, they shall proceed to elect on the second Tuesday after they have had notice of the vacancy."

V. A number of different methods were proposed to the convention. Hon. Henry St. George Tucker, says on this branch of the subject in a speech favoring an amendment to the Federal Constitution, providing for an election of United States Senators by the people:

"Mr. Edmund Randolph, Mr. Charles Pinckney, of of South Carolina, Mr. Alexander Hamilton, Mr. Gerry, and Mr. Wilson, of Pennsylvania, all proposed different methods for the election of Senators. Mr. Randolph proposed in his plan 'that members of the second branch [the Senate] of the National Legislature ought to be elected by those of the first, out of a proper number of persons nominated by the individual legislature.' Mr. Pinckney proposed that the Senate should be chosen by the House of Representatives; and in the draft submitted by Mr. Hamilton it was proposed to elect Senators to hold during good behavior, their election to be made by electors chosen by the people.

"The plans of Mr. Randolph, Mr. Hamilton and Mr. Pinckney were very similar in many respects. They all aimed at taking the election of Senators as far away from the people as it was possible to do, while Mr. Gerry proposed that the Senators should be appointed by the executives of the several States, and Mr. Wilson, of Pennsylvania, and Mr. George Mason, of Virginia, advocated the adoption of the principle for which we contend to-day, the election of Senators by the people. On Mr. Wilson's proposition to elect by the people ten states voted 'nay,' and Pennsylvania alone voted 'yea,' and on the proposition to elect by the Legislatures two states only voted 'nay,' Virginia and Pennsylvania.

"It is evident that those who believed in the theories of Mr. Hamilton, Mr. Randolph, and Mr. Pinckney, as submitted by them, desired that the Senate of the United States should be an oligarchy, an aristocratic oligarchy, some even going to the extent of advocating their appointment or selection for life."

Mr. Gerry says at another time, and it is an interesting point as bearing upon this question:

"The commercial and moneyed interest would be more secure in the hands of the State Legislatures than of the people at large. The former have more sense of character and will be restrained by that from injustice. The people are for paper money when the Legislatures are against it. In Massachusetts the county conventions had declared a wish for a depreciating paper that would sink itself. Besides in some States there are two branches in the Legislature, one of which is somewhat aristocratic. There would, therefore, be so far a better chance of refinement in the choice."

Mr. Pinckney thought—

"That the second branch ought to be permanent and independent, and that the members of it would be rendered more so by receiving their appointments from the State Legislatures."

Mr. Dickinson "had two reasons for his motion," which was to elect by Legislature:

"First, because the sense of the States would be better collected through their governments immediately from the people at large; secondly, because he wished the Senate to consist of the most distinguished characters, distinguished for their rank in life and their weight of property, and bearing as strong a likeness to the British House of Lords as was possible;" and he thought "such characters more likely to be selected by the State Legislatures than in any other mode."

Mr. Wilson, of Pennsylvania, held the view that—

"If we are to establish a national government, that government ought to flow from the people at large. If one branch of it should be chosen by the Legislatures and the other by the people, the two branches would rest on different foundations and dissensions will naturally arise between them. He wished the Senate to be elected by the people as well as the other branch."

Mr. Morris thought that—

"The second branch ought to be composed of men of great and established property, an aristocracy. Men who from pride will support consistency and permanency, and to make them completely independent they must be chosen for life, or they will be a useless body. Such an aristocratic body will keep down the turbulency of democracy; but if you elect them for a shorter period they will be only a name, and we had better be without them. Thus constituted, I hope they will show us the might of aristocracy. History proves, I admit, that the men of large property will uniformly endeavor to establish tyranny. How, then, shall we ward off this evil? Give them the second branch, and you secure their weight for the public good."

That is, give the money power what it asks, and it will be satisfied. So will the highway robber.

I ask attention to the views of a very distinguished Virginian in that convention, no less a person than George Mason, views expressed by him in the Federal convention, and afterwards in the Virginia convention.

"The Senators are chosen for six years; they are not recallable for these six years and are re-eligible at the end of the six years. It stands on a very different ground from the Confederation. By that system they were only elected for one year, might be recalled, and were incapable of re-election. But in the new Constitution instead of being elected for one, they are chosen for six years. They can not be recalled in all that time for any misconduct; and at the end of that long term may again be elected. What will be the operation of this?"

Now mark his prediction:

"Is it not probable that these gentlemen who will be elected Senators, will fix themselves in the Federal town, and become citizens of that town more than of our state? They will purchase a good seat in or near the town and become inhabitants of that place. Will it not be then in the power of the Senate to worry the House of Representatives into anything? They will be a continually existing body. They will exercise those machinations and contrivances which the many have always to fear from the few. The House of Representatives is the only check on the Senate, with their enormous powers. But by that clause you give them the power of worrying the House of Representatives into a compliance with any measure."

"The Senators living on the spot will feel no inconvenience from long sessions, as they will vote themselves handsome pay without incurring any additional expense."

"Your representatives are on a different ground, from their shorter continuance in office. The gentlemen from Georgia are six or seven hundred miles from home and wish to go home. The Senate, taking advantage of this by stopping the other House from adjourning, may worry them into anything. These are my views, and I think the provision not consistent with the usual parliamentary modes."

These extracts develop the fact that there were many in the convention who sought to create in the Senate an aristocratic oligarchy amenable to no power and answerable to no authority.

VI. But there is an element more dangerous to the liberties of the people than that of individual wealth in its influence on the election of Senators. The wonderful growth of our country has been greatly accelerated by the combinations of wealth in corporate forms. These in their proper spheres are to be encouraged rather than condemned; but when they leave their legitimate fields of operation and seek to control, against the interests of the people, the legislation of the country, whether they be banks or railroads, corporations or trusts, or combines, they will meet with the indignant protests of all true friends of the people. The number of employes in their control, the concentration of great wealth in their treasuries, and the "parliamentary favors" which they are able and most willing to bestow, render their advances most enticing and their approaches most insinuating. Their interests are guarded by the ablest men of each community, and, if public rumor be true, they can lay their hands on representatives of the people in many of the Legislatures in the land and claim them as their own.

If the people dare seek relief from their exactions they are met by the agents of the corporations, who attempt to thwart them at every step. All that shrewdness, audacity, and money can suggest is readily at their command. The Legislature is invaded, and the rights of the people give place to the exactions of corporate power; while he who can serve the corporations by his control of a Legislature, by intrigue, artifice, or persuasion, against the demands of the people, is regarded in modern days as "more terrible than any army with banners," and as fully equipped himself for service in the Senate, where in that enlarged field his powers can be utilized for the benefit of the corporations he serves.

The standard for the exalted position of United States Senator is thus debased by corporate influence. The wire-puller and the intriguer are often preferred to the statesman and the patriot, and the proud title of United States Senator has lost much of its power in the suspicions which lurk in the public mind as to the mode, condition, and requirements of their selection.

VII. Of the eighty-eight Senators of the last Senate, who sat and dallied in the midst of commercial misery and industrial distress, that the profits of a market, responsive to their practical moods, might recupe their coffers for moneys expended in purchasing a seat in the Senate; a $ mark may safely be set opposite the names of one-fourth of the members, as indicating the number that now hold seats and owe their election solely to the corrupt use of money. The number is growing! The corruption increases. As it stands, the United States Senate is the representative in our system of government, of Bosses and Boodle. It seems to be an unwritten law of the body, that no matter how serious the charges of corrupt methods used by a Senator or his agents to purchase a seat, the title must not be questioned, and the methods and ugly details of the rascality must not be laid bare. That fraud called "senatorial courtesy" acts as a triple-plated armor to turn aside the most solid truths that crash against this obdurate body and fall harmless. Several attempts have been made to have Congress endorse an amendment to the constitution, providing for an election of Senators by the people. These worthy and commendable attempts to purge the dross from the Senate in the furnace of popular approval, have all perished and found a burial in the senatorial graveyard, without the formality of a funeral or the mock reverence that could conceal the purpose in the hypocrisy of an epitaph. The silence of the Senate in this matter is an evidence of conscious guilt, and a sign that shame is not dead. It is a matter of congratulation that since the advent of boodlers in the United States Senate, no man in all this broad land, of any character and standing, has been found who dared brave public ridicule by denying the existence of these practices, and no one has presumed to attempt a defense of these methods. It shows that the public conscience is not dead. The people are honest, and the guilty ones dread the dawn of that day when both shall be aroused.

CHAPTER III.

"BOSSES," "BOODLE" AND THE "MACHINE."

"WE are highwaymen. We stop stages and carriages on the road, with masks on, and kill the people and take their watches and money."

"Must we always kill the people?"

"Oh, certainly. It's best. Some authorities think different, but mostly it's considered best to kill them. Except some that you bring to the cave here and keep them till they're ransomed."

"Ransomed? What's that?"

"I don't know. But that's what they do. I've seen it in books; and so, of course, that's what we've got to do."

"But how can we do it if we don't know what it is?"

"Why, blame it all, we've got to do it. Don't I tell you it's in the books? Do you want to go to doing different from what's in the books, and get things all muddled up?"

"Oh, that's all very fine to say, Tom Sawyer, but how in the nation are these fellows going to be ransomed if we don't know how to do it to them? That's the thing I want to get at. Now what do you reckon it is?"

"Well, I don't know. But per'aps if we keep them till they're ransomed, it means that we keep them till they're dead."

"Now, that's something like. That'll answer. Why couldn't you said that before? We'll keep them till they're ransomed to death and a bothersome lot they'll be, too, eating up everything and always trying to get loose."

"How you talk, Ben Rogers. How can they get loose when there's a guard over them, ready to shoot them down if they move a peg?"

"A guard! Well, that is good. So somebody's got to set up all night and never get any sleep, just so as to watch them. I think that's foolishness. Why can't a body take a club and ransomed them as soon they get here?"

"Because it ain't in the books so—that's why. Now, Ben Rogers, do you want to do things regular, or don't you?—that's the idea. Don't you reckon that the people that made the books knows what's the correct thing to do? Do you reckon you can learn 'em anything? Not by a good deal. No, sir, we'll just go on and ransomed them in the regular way."—*Huckleberry Finn*.

I. The words, "Bosses," "Boodle" and "Machine," are not new, but these terms, as applied to our politics, are of recent origin, and the need of such words grew out of the existing conditions in our political affairs. The word Boss, is a United States word, belonging solely to our language. It was taken from an old Dutch word, *Baas*, meaning a master workman or superintendent. As used in connection with politics, it means one who controls and directs a part or all of the machinery in politics. There are all kinds, grades, sizes, prices and styles of political bosses; from the little fellow who controls his precinct, in city, town or county, to those big fellows who manipulate parties in state and nation.

II. The word "boodle," is a new one. It does not appear in any of the old dictionaries. Its origin is only explained by the most recent works. The word was first used by the press in 1884–5. It was probably taken from the word "caboodle," or "capoodle," as used in some sections, and meaning an entire lot. It originated and grew out of the wholesale purchase of the Ohio Legislature, in 1884–5, by which Henry B. Payne secured his seat in the United States Senate. The word "bribery," would not cover a wholesale transaction. Bribery is a retail word, not meant to cover large transactions and a gigantic piece of rascality, and the American mind, quick to coin words to meet emergencies, gave us the word "boodle." This word, as used now, means money raised to be used for dishonest and corrupt purposes in politics. The "bosses" and "boodle" combined, make the "machine," which is the men and methods used to accomplish certain results inside of party organizations. The objects and purposes of the political "machine" are always selfish. The "machine" is a political trust, organized to benefit one man or a few, and to defeat an honest expression of the rank and file of a party, and to defy and set at naught the will of the people. It is a method resorted to by wealthy, corrupt and designing men, to secure office, power and honors, which would be denied them, did they make a frank avowal of their purposes and an open appeal to the people. It is not possible to buy all the people or even a majority. To openly attempt it, would be disastrous to Bosses and Boodlers. The lion of public indignation must not be aroused, for if it is, the occupation of the Bosses would be gone, and the Bosses would go with it. For these reasons the places and purposes of the party Bosses are not openly avowed, but they are hidden and masked behind fair promises, and fierce declarations of party principles and fealty. When the direst deviltry is to be perpetrated, the greatest cunning is resorted to, to dissemble and deceive. Men are selected for their character, ability and prominence to give utterance to "key notes," and to guide the deliberations, while unwary and unsuspecting lambs are led to the precipice and pushed over, in a drove. Politics under our system presents more opportunities for developing and exercising the innate cussedness of man, than any system that has ever been devised. It is a rich field, full of endless combinations and surprises, for a display of all the ingenuity that the human intellect is capable of. There is a fascination about the turmoil and pursuit of politics, that cannot be described. There are temptations in the flowery fields of politics that few are able to resist. There is a demoralization that is universal, and which taints all that touch the game. The world to the end may applaud the brilliant and successful participants, but they soon forget the many who fall by the wayside, and these, whose remnant of conscience survives the ordeal, never forgive themselves for their loss of self-respect. If this is a plain and fair statement of political organizations and politicians, as they exist to-day and as we see them; it may be well to make some simple and elemental statements about party organizations, that the reader may be prepared to understand and believe what is to follow.

III. A history of the evolution of political organizations, under our form of government, is not necessary for the purposes of this work. At present we have two great political organizations, that represent the antagonistic forces, that keep our institutions in a healthy state of activity. What one of the great parties favors the other opposes, but both have one object in common, *i. e.*, both want the offices, and to secure these, seems to be the chief object of the present organizations. Around the main tents of the great political circuses, are a number of side shows, in which the mastodon's tooth, the bearded lady, the india-rubber man and other freaks and relics are displayed. Our government is an anomaly among the governments of the earth; inasmuch at it is a government based upon the popular will, and it is a government of the minority, as a majority of the people have never supported any party or endorsed any principle advocated except the preservation of the Union.

Notwithstanding the great distrust of the people, among the authors of our constitution and the founders of the government, the tendency from the first has been steadily toward the recognition of the rights of the individual in our political and social fabric. In his masterly work on "Social Evolution," Benjamin Kidd says:

"The progress towards individual liberty, which is known to the student of jurisprudence as the movement from status to contract, and which has thus, as it were, become registered in our laws, has a deeper meaning than at first sight appears. Closely regarding, as a whole, the process of change which has been going on in our western civilization, the evolutionist begins to perceive that it essentially consists in the slow breaking-up of that military type of society which reached its highest development in, although it did not disappear with, the Roman Empire. Throughout the history of the western people there is one central fact which underlies all the shifting scenes which move across the pages of the historian. The political history of the centuries so far may be summed up in a single sentence—it is the story of the political and the social enfranchisement of the masses of the people hitherto universally excluded from participation in the rivalry of existence on terms of equality. This change, it is seen, is being accomplished against the most prolonged and determined resistance at many points, and under innumerable forms, of the power-holding classes, which obtained, under an earlier constitution of society, the influence which they have hitherto, to a large extent, although in gradually diminishing measure, continued to enjoy. The point at which the process tends to culminate is a condition of society in which the whole mass of the excluded people will be at last brought into the rivalry of existence on a footing of equality of opportunity.

"The steps in this process have been slow, to a degree, but the development has never been interrupted, and it probably will not be until it has reached that point up to which it has always been the inherent tendency of the principle of our civilization to carry it.

"The first great stage in the advance was accomplished when slavery, for the first time in history, became extinct in Europe somewhere about the fourteenth century. From this point onward the development has continued under many forms amongst the people included in our civilization—locally accelerated or retarded by various causes, but always in progress.

"Amongst all the Western people there has been a slow but sure restriction of the absolute power possessed under military rule by the head of the state. The gradual decay of feudalism has been accompanied by the transfer of a large part of the rights, considerably modified, of the feudal lord to the landowning, and later to the capitalist classes which succeeded them. But we find these rights undergoing a continuous process of restriction, as the classes which inherit them have been compelled to extend political power in ever increasing measure to those immediately below. As the rights and powers of the upper classes have been gradually curtailed, the great slowly formed middle class has, in its turn, found itself confronted with the same developmental tendency. Wider and wider the circle of political influence has gradually extended. Whether the progress has been made irregularly amid the throes of revolution, or more regularly in the orderly course of continuous legislative enactment, it has never ceased. The nineteenth century alone has witnessed an enormous extension of political power to the masses amongst most of the advanced people included in our civilization. In England the list of measures, aiming either directly or indirectly at the emancipation and the raising of the lower classes of people, that have been placed on the statute book in the lifetime of even the present generation, is an imposing one, and it continues yearly to be added to. Last of all it may be perceived that in our own day, amid all the conflict of rival parties, and all the noise and exaggeration of heated combatants, we are definitely entering on a stage when the advancing party is coming to set clearly before it, as the object of endeavor, the ideal of a state of society in which there shall be at last no law-protected, power-holding class on the one side, and no excluded and disinherited masses on the other—a stage in which, for a long period to come, legislation will aim at securing to all the members of the community the right to be admitted to the rivalry of life, as far as possible, on a footing of equality of opportunity."

IV. This law, or tendency, does not seem to hold good as to political organizations! Here the disposition is to distrust the people—the masses—and concentrate all control and power in the hands of the bosses. The "refining" process, such as our fathers thought necessary in selecting officers, has been perfected, and is one of the most potent factors in a perfect political machine! Laws have been passed and perfected until the citizen can cast his vote in peace and safety and go to bed with a reasonable hope of having it counted, but outside of the mere matter of voting, as a rule, he has no voice, no vote and no influence in shaping the policy and selecting the nominees of his party. This is all done for him by the Boss, through the aid of Boodle and the Machinery. A partisan is not expected to think! A day is fixed for a party primary. It is held under the law, and conducted by the regular election officers. Every member of the organization, who is willing to abide the result, may vote! Delegates are chosen to a state or county convention. If to a state convention, these delegates select men to prepare a platform of principles. They nominate a ticket. They select members of an organization by congressional districts which is called a central committee. This committee selects an executive or campaign committee.

In a county convention the same process is gone through with on a smaller scale. As a rule, the members of a party have no voice in choosing candidates, or naming members of the various committees that present principles and provide the issues and conduct the campaign. The committees are the fly-wheel of the machine, and these the Boss, by the use of patronage and Boodle, always controls! To permit them to be chosen by the people would jeopardize success and defeat the nicely prepared plans of the "Bosses." We have county committees, senatorial committees, congressional committees, and state committees, all chosen by delegates, which the people are permitted to vote for, and these have general powers and similar duties. They fix the time and place of meeting, and arrange the basis of representation to the various conventions, and this is all done to suit the pleasure and convenience of the Bosses, and not those of the people. There is one other duty, which custom has made a committeeman believe is his sole and sovereign right, and that is to receive and disburse the "Boodle" in his district. He is in touch with all the delicate machinery in his special territory. He knows every man and his worth, and how much he can spend and whether he will spend it. This last is a very important item, as it has been estimated as a rule, that not more than 75 per cent. of the money, set aside to corrupt the people, ever reaches the spot. Many committeemen are patriots. They keep the money themselves rather than see it used to debauch others. This is their reward for services rendered. The Boss merely holds them responsible for results, and he dare not question too closely as to methods. The average committeeman has a keen scent for "Boodle." He can feel the magnetic thrill when the first "bar'l" is opened and the golden grease begins to flow from headquarters. He is first on the ground and most exhortant in demands, and specific as to the needs of money, in large bundles, in his locality. During the progress of the campaign, he becomes the bane of the campaign manager's life, and is a perpetual menace to his party's success. But he is a necessary evil that cannot be dispensed with.

V. When the nominations are made, the platform adopted, the flag unfurled and the battle set in array, the average party man has nothing to do but shut his eyes, and yell for the whole outfit. He may know of his personal knowledge that one or all of the candidates are dishonest, and nominations were secured by dishonest and corrupt methods, against which his manhood revolts, but he is helpless. He cannot protest. He must remain silent. To question is treason. He is left with one consolation to quiet and soothe his conscience. His scoundrel is better than the rascal on the other ticket. He don't want to bolt. He cannot give up the party of his convictions. He cannot join any of the parties of the cranks and isms. He does not want to loose his vote. As the fight progresses the old feeling comes back. His loyalty to his party organization is aroused by some able leader, that he has long known and always trusted, and he votes the old ticket from top to bottom, Bosses, Boodle and all, and trusts to time and the future to correct the evils that disgrace his organization, and to remove the Bosses and their methods. The Boss smiles. The returns at the election being a consummation of all his well laid plans. He is fortified by one more victory. The end grows. The abject cowardice of the honest citizen, and blind partisan, makes possible a condition in politics, which he deplores but dare not denounce.

VI. Parties spring into existence around some great central principle. Ideas cluster around this central force, and men rally to its support until the principle is crystalized into law, and becomes a fact. No party long survives the realization of the purpose that called it into existence. Decay begins when the consummation is achieved. When a party is young and its followers are fired by the noble enthusiasm of its principles, money cannot buy its partisans or pervert them. They are not for sale. But when a party is held together by its memories of the past, and its leaders are guided by the cohesive power of spoils, then an opportune field presents itself for the exercise of the talents of the Boss, and Boodle is necessary to party success. Under the earlier and better conditions of party organization and existence, the ambitions of the young and talented are aroused, and avenues of office and promotion present themselves as a reward for their services and affording opportunity for the exercise of high mental qualities with which nature has endowed them. They bear the brunt of the battle. They carry the banner against hopeless odds. They give their time, their money and their talent freely, to aid the cause they believe in. A generation of great men often spring into existence with the birth of a party. They grow with its growth. They achieve greatness with its success, and when they have run their course and pass away, the party passes away.

But Boodle and Bosses, while they achieve temporary success of a doubtful character, never made a party great or insured it lasting success. It never can. It never has. It never will. When Boodle arrogantly stalks upon the stage, the avenues of advancement are closed against the young and gifted who seek promotion through honorable avenues. The belief is now prevalent that no one can succeed in politics without money, and this fact, which few dispute, drives the most desirable class of our young citizens away from any active participation in our political affairs.

VII. There are honest and legitimate uses to which money may be put in a well conducted campaign, such as printing, postage, telegraphing, clerk hire, speaker's expenses, etc. I speak of campaigns as conducted by the Democracy in Ohio. I know but little about those conducted by any other party, except as the signs were made manifest during a canvass. Formerly a host of able and unselfish speakers volunteered their services. Their expenses were paid by the local committees. They would have scorned to ask or receive pay, but when "Boodle" made its appearance, there was a change. No one has any time now to give to his party outside of his own locality. All expect to be remunerated for time spent and services rendered.

Speakers of national reputation are employed by national committees and receive a stipulated price, as a rule, for the number of speeches or the length of time employed. In the presidential campaign of 1880, Col. Frank McKenney, of Piqua, Ohio, was Chairman of the Executive Committee. A number of men now prominent were sent into the state to take part in the canvass, among these a man who is now a United States Senator, and two, Burke Cochran and John Fellows, who have since become famous, and have been members of Congress. It was reported and generally believed, that a large sum of money had been sent into Ohio by the national committee, upon representations made on the strength of the poll, that the state could be carried with "Boodle." Either the money did not reach the spot, or its purpose was defeated by publicity.

But the foreign speakers seemed to be the first to learn that a "bar'l" had been opened. The United States Senator was at Marietta to meet an engagement, and refused to fill his appointments until money was sent. He got the money and continued to run his wind-mill. John Fellows was at Hillsboro when he made a demand for money. He sent in from this place a bill for a suit of clothes.

Since that campaign the professional "spell-binder" has been a luxury in Ohio, and he takes no promises to pay but demands his money in advance. Since men have ceased to be patriotic, and give their services in any capacity to their party for the love of the cause, it requires money, and plenty of it, even to set the wheels of the party machinery in motion, and it requires a great deal more to keep them moving.

In the campaign of 1867, when the 15th amendment was the issue and R. B. Hayes was the Republican candidate for Governor and was opposed by Allen G. Thurman on the Democratic ticket, the Republicans elected their state ticket by a small majority, and the Democrats carried the legislature, and Allen G. Thurman was chosen United States Senator; neither campaign committee spent over $5,000 and the Democratic campaign fund was less than this. In 1883, Geo. Hoadley spent three times this amount to buy the Democratic nomination for Governor, and defeated Durbin Ward, the honest choice of his party.

VIII. There are only two ways of raising the large campaign funds, now so fashionable and so necessary. One is by assessing the members of the party who hold office and those who are candidates, and by contributions from those who are willing and anxious to hold office. Usually the managers expect those who hold office in counties that give the party a safe majority, to defray the expenses of the campaign, and send a contribution to the state committee. If there is any money to spare, above the ordinary expenses of the campaign, it is sent to the minority counties, to aid in "organizing the party and in getting the vote to the polls." This is the official language of the campaign circular, and it would make a chairman writhe in agony like Hercules in his poisoned shirt, did he suspect for one moment, that one dollar of the money sent out, would be used to currupt one of our noble lords and sovereigns, the citizens.

There is no data to show the exact number of men that hold places under our state constitution and laws. It is a safe guess to say that there are 100,000 Democrats and Republicans who hold places in Ohio, and form part of the Machine. This reaches from the constable in a precinct to the governor of the state, and includes the school system and the judiciary. There are 88 counties in the state, and from 14 to 20 townships in a county. There are 200 township, municipal and county offices in the smallest counties, and from 3,000 to 5,000 in the larger counties, counting the cities of Cincinnati, Cleveland, Columbus, Toledo and Dayton, with a proportionate number in the counties between these extremes.

There are justices of the peace, constables, judges of election, school directors, assessors, probate judges, clerks, commissioners, auditors, coroners, surveyors, prosecuting attorneys, infirmary directors, in the townships and county organizations, and in the municipal governments there are mayors, police boards, members of council, etc., and most of these are elected on the tickets of one or the other of the two leading parties; and in the government we have the state officers with their assistants and clerks, and the state institutions. All of these are expected to pay tribute to their party organization in hard cash, and to render election services before and during the election. The money contributed is given by wealthy men who are looking ahead for honors, or from corporate interests or combinations at home or abroad, that expect favors and consideration in state and national legislation. Sometimes it is expensive, but those who contribute are blessed and are rarely disappointed.

Under the laws passed in Ohio, known as the Australian ballot system, the expense of printing tickets is now borne by the state, and there is no longer any need of money for ward "healers," "knockers" and "strikers." This saves a large sum of money, for these men cost from $2 to $20 each, according to their "pull;" all now is done decently and in order. There are no scenes of violence at the polls. Men buy and sell votes in the most respectable manner. When a contest is close and votes are needed, under our present law and order system, a responsible man is placed in every precinct.

When the purchasable commodity is located, a regular price is agreed on for votes. Sometimes a pool is made and one man makes a bargain to deliver a certain number of votes for a stated sum. He is shown the poll and agrees for so much a head, to deliver more votes than the canvass shows. But how do they know when a man sells his vote under the Australian system? One of the judges or clerks is called by the voter into the booth to prepare his ticket. If he has agreed to sell his vote for the whole ticket, or only one candidate, the ticket is fixed as he requests. When the ballot is cast, a signal is given to the watcher and the cash is paid for the vote as promised. This is an evasion of a very strict law, but not a violation. As the system is now perfected, we find the tyranny of party complete. It is absolute. Bolting is the only remedy for the disease.

We have a government of Boodle, by Boodle and for Boodle. The man who sells and the man who buys, are criminals in the eyes of the law. The man who supplies the money is the master knave and scoundrel. But he is so many degrees removed from the crime and the criminals that he can never be reached. This evil will continue until a law can be framed and enforced, that will put a convict's stripes on some vulgar and brazen millionaire, and thus brand the Boss Boodler as the most dangerous criminal in our civilization and the greatest foe to our free institutions. We do not expect the day will ever dawn when poor, weak human nature will be above temptation, but we do expect to see the time at a very early date, when our legislators will cease to frame laws to catch flies, and when an enlightened and aroused public opinion will make laws, and enforce them, and then Boodlers will become infamous, and will find their places in the felon's cell, and not disgrace our people and scandalize a nation by the open purchase of seats in the United States Senate.

When this time comes party organizations will be reformed, and all power will spring directly from the people, and United States Senators and the President of the same, and all other officers, will be chosen by the people. If the people cannot be trusted, this last attempt at a free and popular form of government is a failure, and the sooner that is demonstrated the better for mankind. One fact has been made painfully apparent by recent events: our government exists and is controlled solely for the benefit of wealth, and not for the benefit of men. In the midst of a civil war, men are taken from homes and altars and their lives are sacrificed to preserve the nation. But the same government which can take the lives of the poor men to preserve it, dare not touch the surplus of the wealthy. In times of profound peace the highest tribunal in the land, denies the right of Congress to tax the surplus of the rich to pay the interest on a war debt, and to defray the expense of government. The Court appointed for life, legislates and defeats the will of the representatives chosen by the people. The Court proclaims the doctrine that the burdens of taxation must fall upon labor, upon the necessities of life, upon consumption and the needs of the poor, but the surplus of wealth in every form must be sacredly guarded from the vulgar touch and impudent inquisition of the tax gatherer. This echo from the golden gong by the high-priests in the temple of justice, chords with the chimes of corruption that has placed the golden dollar mark upon a fourth of the seats in the United States Senate.

If a hungry and aggrieved workingman disturbs this profound peace, which he has made possible by his bravery and sacrifice in war; if in his mistaken zeal for wages that will enable him to live and feed his babies, he engages in strikes, and indulges in riots and excesses, let a President violate the constitution and the rights of the states by calling out the military to kill; let the judges hurl the indignation of organized wealth at disorganized and starving labor, by an injunction, which, if ignored, means imprisonment for offending judicial tyranny; but let no virtuous citizen, no honest and indignant son of toil, try to turn this last instrument of oppression in government, by praying an injunction against a corrupt millionaire, who is debauching the people and buying their representatives, by the open and scandalous purchase of a seat in the United States Senate.

If some man should be insane enough to apply to

a United States Judge for an injunction to prevent the purchase of a senatorship, would he get a hearing? Or would the Judge send him to the Lebanon jail or the nearest asylum? Within three months we have seen a judge rule two different ways on the income tax. This change of mind has been heralded as an evidence of courageous conviction and the highest patriotism. When a member of the Ohio Legislature changes his mind on the eve of a senatorial caucus, he is justly suspected of bribery.

The tendency in our government to-day is not in keeping with the spirit of the age and its progress. Money and not man is the beacon light toward which too many are striving. There must be a speedy and a peaceable adjustment of our laws and our political conditions, to meet the just demands of the masses, or something will snap; and when the cable breaks some one is liable to be bodily hurt. Let us hope that the day is not distant, when reason, justice and honesty will prevail over Bosses and Boodle, and their methods, in all sections of our land, among all classes of our people and all stations in our official life.

CHAPTER IV.

FROM BUCKEYE TO BOODLE.

"THE most effective speakers and writers are not those who tell all they think or feel, but those who, by maintaining an austere conscientiousness of phrase, leave on their hearers and readers the impression of reserved power. On the other hand, if we do the work of a pistol with a twenty-four pounder, or kill cock robins with Gatling guns — and, when anything more formidable is to be destroyed, touch off the fusee of a volcano — we shall find, when we come to the real tug of war, that our instruments of offense are weak, worn out and worthless. Great bastions of military strength must lie at rest in times of peace, that they may be able to execute their destructive agencies in times of war; and so let it be with the superlatives of our tongue. Never call on the 'tenth legion' or 'the old guard' except on occasions corresponding to the dignity and weight of those tremendous forces. Say plain things in a plain way, and then, when you have occasion to send a sharp arrow at your enemy, you will not find your quiver empty of shafts which you wasted before they were wanted."— *Words: Their Uses and Abuses.*

Ohio was the 17th admitted to the family of states that comprised the union known as the United States of America. It was the first child of the Ordinance of 1787, the greatest product of human experience and statesmanship. This instrument, so justly lauded, was the work of a paid lobby*, and dictated by the agent of a paid company that was enabled to make its own terms owing to the impoverished condition of the treasury of the confederation, and the suffering and distress that followed the war of the revolution; the result of a worthless paper money that destroyed the credit of the colonies. Ohio was the first government ever created for a people before they inhabitated the territory for which the government was created. Under the Ordinance of 1787, and the contract with the Ohio Land Company, our government first established the principle of deriving a revenue from the sale of its public domain known then as the "back country." In his "Commonwealth of Ohio," Hon. Rufus King, in commenting upon the Ordinance of 1787, says:

"In the two concluding articles it was ordained:

"'There shall be neither slavery nor involuntary servitude in said territory, otherwise than in punishment of crime;' and that 'religion, morality, and knowledge, being essential to good government and the happiness of mankind, shall forever be encouraged.' These were placed by the ordinance as among 'the fundamental principles of civil and religious liberty which formed the basis whereon these republics, their laws, and constitutions, are erected.'

* See Dr. Manasseh Cutler's Journal, Vol. I, Chap. VI.

"The men who settled Ohio believed this, and proved it by the care with which the principles summed up and consecrated in the Ordinance were preserved and handed down in the Constitutions of both 1802 and 1851; especially in the articles prohibiting slavery and favoring the encouragement of religion, morality, and knowledge as the means of government.

"The former is that upon which the people of 'these republics' have been the most intent during the century since the Ordinance and the Constitution were framed, and which by a convulsive effort have been laid at rest.

"The other principle has not been sustained; indeed, it may be said to have lost much of its force, under powerful foreign influences which have asserted themselves in American politics and laws. But that this declaration was, at the time, the fixed and general sentiment of the American people and statemen, is undeniable. General Washington and Dr. Franklin have left no uncertainty as to this, and there were no better exponents. The colonies, in fact, were founded upon it and for its sake. It became ingrained in the very fibre of those indigenous governments and institutions which were a century and a half silently growing up to form the American republic. It was the fervent intermingling of the spirit of liberty with this reverence for religion and morality, as being the 'basis of good government and the happiness of mankind,' that first struck the attention of European patriots, and of which De Tocqueville was so keenly observant in his view of American democracy.

"Whether it is not time that American statesmen

were heeding it, let wise men consider. It is not safe to forsake the customs and principles by which a people has risen to greatness. Nor did a people ever fail of enduring prosperity and happiness by the ways pointed out in the Ordinance of 1787. Democracy, or democratic institutions, can not rise above their foundation. In their nature they can not be enduring without a public opinion powerfully rooted and reinforced in religion and morality."

II. Ohio, the name given to the territory and rising state, by act of Congress, is an Indian word, meaning beautiful. In 1784 Congress adopted a plan for a temporary form of government for the "back country." It was proposed to divide the territory west of the Alleghany Mountains, and north and south of the Ohio River, and east of the Mississippi, into seventeen new states or divisions, by lines of latitude two degrees apart; to be intersected by two meridians of longtitude to be drawn north and south of the mouth of the Big Kanawha River and at the Falls of the Ohio River, where Louisville is now located. These new creations were to go down in history by such classical titles as Sylvania, Michigania, Chersonesus, Assenisipia, Metropotomia, Illinoia, Saratoga, Washington, Polypotomia, and Pilisipia, the latter being a name attempted to be given the Ohio River. Mr. Jefferson's plan was recommitted to the committee, and the latter part was never adopted, otherwise what is now known as Ohio would have been divided between the state of Metropotomia, Washington and Pilisipia.

III. The origin of the term "Buckeye," as applied to the state and its people, is unknown. Several explanations of a learned and interesting character have been made, but none of them are satisfactory or conclusive.

The Ordinance of 1787 contained a proviso that when the population of the territory reached "5,000 free white male inhabitants," it should be entitled to a representation in Congress, and a territorial legislature might be chosen by the people. A census of the territory in 1798 showed a population of 5,000, and Governor St. Clair issued a proclamation for an election of members to a legislative body, and to be chosen for every five hundred of the population. At this election counties elected representatives as follows: Washington County (the Muskingum) 2; Hamilton (the Miamis) 7; Ross (the Scioto) 4; Adams (the Virginia Military District) 2; Jefferson (Upper Ohio) 1; Wayne (Detroit, Mich.) 3; St. Clair and Randolph (Illinois) 1 each; and Knox (Indiana) 1; total, 22. Governor St. Clair transferred the seat of government to the "town opposite the mouth of Licking," Losantiville, in 1799, and convened the new legislative body to meet in this place, Sept. 23, 1799. The Governor, who seemed to have considered his own will and wishes, as the embodiment of all the constitution and laws that the people of the territory needed, had provided a seal for the virgin state; but as every thing that he did was looked upon either as a blunder or a crime, this ambitious attempt to give an official emblem to the executive department, which was all there was of the government, was met with ridicule. The device on the seal was intended to represent a buckeye tree, standing erect in the background, with another tree felled in the foreground and cut up into logs. This Latin motto encircled this scene from the pioneer forest: "*Meliorem Lapsa Locavit*," which means, "He planted one better than the fallen." It has been claimed that this device on this seal gave the appellation of "Buckeyes" to Ohio and her people. Cynics, however, who disliked Governor St. Clair, and disliked the buckeye tree, deeming both worthless, used the seal to belittle the Governor, and made the term of "Buckeye" one of disdain. One of the most notable characters in the new country was a man named Chapman, who was known as "Johnny Appleseed." He was a harmless sort of a person, but he had a mission. He went about with some Swedenborgian tracts and a bag of apple seed, and planted both where he thought they would grow, and thus rendered an undoubted service to generations yet unborn. He was a character typical of the age, and a bloodless hero, who deserves a monument, at the hands of the people of a great empire, to commemorate his unselfish labors. It is doubtful whether there was sentiment enough in Governor St. Clair's composition to gather the poetic idea for his seal from the life of "Johnny Appleseed."

IV. *Pavio Ohioensis*, the Ohio buckeye, or American horse-chestnut, is a native of the Ohio Valley. It is one of the most beautiful of our native trees. The trunk rarely exceeds twelve or fifteen inches in diameter. It grows to the height of twenty-five or thirty feet, and the branches of the tree, with the dark foliage, present a symmetrical form that is very graceful and pleasing to the eye. The trunk of the tree is rather smooth and blackish, and the wood is white, very soft and almost useless, even for fuel. The bloom of the tree is brilliant. The flowers, in the wild state, are among the first that bloom in the spring, and are collected in white bunches. The chestnut grows in waxen-like, prickly capsules, and ripens and falls with the early frosts. It is as large as a walnut, and resembles the ordinary chestnut very much; the shell being of a dark, rich brown, with a light spot, making it resemble the beautiful eye of the deer, which fact has given it the name of "Buckeye."

The rapid growth, dense foliage, beauty of its flowers, and hardy character, make it a very fine shade tree, but the fact that the buckeye is poisonous and dangerous to animal life, has brought it into discredit, and it is rapidly dying out, and like other wild children of the forest, it is fading before the rapid strides of civilization. The chief use our pioneer fathers found for the buckeye was to make troughs out of the soft wood, to catch the sap from the sugar maple when it began to run, and when not used for this they made convenient cradles for a new generation of giants which came to complete the foundations of a great state. The term "Buckeye" continued to be used as one of doubtful compliment for forty years after the territory became a state. At a banquet given in Cincinnati, along in the forties, in celebrating the forty-fourth anniversary of the admission of Ohio into the Union, Dr. Daniel Drake, one of the ablest, cleverest and most useful men of his day and age, made a speech on the "Buckeye," and he held to the idea that the term was first used in ridicule.

S. P. Hildreth, the first historian of the state and the settlement at Marietta by the Ohio Company, relates an incident that gives another aspect to the origin and use of the word, and makes it a title of honor from its first use. The first company of settlers under the grant made by Congress to the Ohio Company, reached Marietta in the spring of 1788, with a government made to order, and a full outfit of officers. The first court of the new territory, which was also the legislature and the governor's council or cabinet, convened with great pomp, on Sept. 2, 1788. A procession was formed consisting of judges, a detail of officers of the army from Fort Harmar, members of the bar, citizens, and the governor and clergymen. These were headed by the high sheriff, Col. Ebenezer Sproat. He was a splendid specimen of manhood, over six feet high, well proportioned, and of commanding presence. He carried a naked sword, and so impressed a number of Indians, who were present, by his voice and bearing, that one of them exclaimed in admiration, "Hetuck!" or "Big Buckeye." This term was applied to Col. Sproat until his death, but the name did not become general in its application to the people of the state until the famous "hard cider and log cabin" campaign of Gen. Wm. Harrison, in 1840, when he was the candidate of the Whig Party for the Presidency, and was elected.

Gen. Harrison was the first hero, and was the idol of the people of the northwestern territory. In fifty years, from his advent as a young officer of the line, he had filled every position in civil and military life. In the one he had been secretary, governor and representative of the territory and state in Congress. He had served his state as a member of the United States Senate. In the army he had filled every position with honor, from an obscure lieutenant to a successful commander. In the western mind, and to those who served under him, he was the military man of the age, and the chief figure in the war with Great Britain. He was serving as clerk of Hamilton County when chosen to lead the Whigs in what appeared to be a hopeless contest. A sneer changed the whole aspect of the campaign and gave the Whigs a battle-cry that led them to victory. A Democratic paper's slur in saying that Gen. Harrison was "better fitted to sit in a log cabin and drink hard cider than rule in the White House," aroused the pride of the people of the northwest, who had but once before been honored by having one of their citizens chosen to lead a great party in a contest for the "highest office in the gift of a free people." The Buckeye log cabin on wheels, decorated with coon skins and strings of buckeyes, and a barrel of hard cider inside, made its appearance as a campaign argument. Buckeye canes, buckeye badges and buckeye poetry grew and blossomed and bore fruit in every township. Gifted Tom Corwin was a candidate for governor in that famous campaign, and the poet told us that

"Tom Corwin is a Buckeye Boy
Who stands not for the pay."

The Buckeye not only became the badge of a party in a great campaign, but the slogan that led to success; and that victory wiped away the stain of derision that formerly attached to the name, and henceforth the term "Buckeye" was one of honor, that neither state nor people have been ashamed to acknowledge. In the fifties, Samuel Sullivan Cox, better known as "Sunset," made a tour of Europe, and gave the name an honorable place in literature by an interesting book on his travels, which he entitled: "The Buckeye Abroad." A painful contrast is presented when we consider the methods and elements in the "log cabin," of 1840, and the "boodle" campaigns of a later date.

V. George Washington was captivated with the beauties, and impressed with the wealth and possibilities of the Ohio Valley, from the first time he saw it, as a young man, acting as a special messenger for the British army, and as a surveyor and prospector. He was granted a tract of 10,000 acres along the Ohio, in West Virginia, between the mouths of the Little and Great Kanawha rivers, and in 1773 he issued a circular from his home "near Alexandria, Va.," calling attention to the natural advantages of these lands, and offering to sell or lease the same to settlers upon moderate terms. He was the first to point out the advantages of inland navigation, and suggested the possibility of connecting the headwaters of the rivers flowing into the Ohio with those emptying into Lake Erie. In the dark hours of the revolution, Washington never despaired. The "back country" offered to him a safe refuge from the victorious arms of Great Britain. Amidst the gloom of defeat, and the sufferings of the little band that shivered around the fires of Valley Forge in the winter of 1777, the question of submission was discussed by the army, from the private's camp-fire to the General's table, and when George Washington was asked: "If we are driven from the Atlantic border, what is to be done?" He replied: "We will retire to the Valley of the Ohio, and there be free." When Continental money was almost worthless, it was Washington that induced Congress, as early as Sept. 20, 1776, to provide for generous bounties in land to those who served in the army. After the war he lost no opportunity in urging upon Congress the necessary action in redeeming both the worthless Continental scrip and the pledges of Congress paid and made to the soldier, by providing that he might settle in the "back country." The Ohio Company of Associates of the New England States was composed largely of revolutionary soldiers, which secured the tract of land in Ohio by land bounties and by the payment of Continental scrip, worth about eight cents on the dollar. In organizing the Ohio Land Company, Dr. Manasseh Cutler, who was a Congregational minister and had served as a chaplain in the revolutionary army, was very particular in choosing his "associates." He did not fancy the idea of having in the new colony "the people from the southward." The Puritan's children, who had settled in bleak New England to escape persecution for opinion's sake, still looked with distrust upon the offspring of the Cavalier, and the descendants of a people who had left England by request of the courts to reside in Virginia, both temporarily or for life, as the case might be. But the law of heredity does not always work along well-established lines, or according to well-defined laws; as yet this science is only a guess; as the waters of a running stream are said to drop all impurities in two miles, so humanity seems capable of refreshing itself in each succeeding generation. Crime is a disease. A product of unhealthy physical conditions and debasing surroundings. Environment has more to do with making criminals than ancestry. As a rule, men do not commit crime when their stomachs are full. In a few years the "people from the southward," whom Dr. Cutler did not think desirable as members of the new state he and his associates were about to launch upon the stormy ocean of time, were destined to become the controlling force in the government. It was the Virginians in the Scioto Valley that hastened the formation of the state and its admission to the Union, and in 1802, Dr. Manasseh Cutler, as a member of Congress from Massachusetts, and the successor of Nathan Dane, who claimed to be the author of the Ordinance of 1787, was one of the few that voted against admitting the first state under that ordinance, and which he and his associates in the Ohio Company had founded fifteen years before.

VI. Ohio was the gateway to the west. The state has the largest and most convenient navigable water-front of any state in the Union. Lake Erie connects with the Atlantic and a chain of lakes whose annual tonnage is greater than that of our ocean ports. The Ohio River skirts the entire southern border of the state and connects with the vast population of the Mississippi Valley and the Gulf. These water-ways, in days when primitive methods of travel prevailed, afforded great advantages, and were eagerly sought by the first settlers and followed by the steady stream of emigration that flowed westward.

The advantages for home and happiness offered by the ordinance of '87, and the promise of government aid and protection, attracted the hardy and best people from all sections of the colonies and many from abroad. Judge Burnet, one of the early Judges of the Northwestern territory, in his excellent and invaluable "Notes," says: "The early adventurers of the Northwestern territory, were generally the men who had spent the prime of their lives in the War of Independence. Many of them had exhausted their fortunes in maintaining the desperate struggle, and retired to the wilderness to conceal their poverty and avoid comparisons mortifying to their pride while struggling to maintain their families and improve their condition."

In reply to a letter written by Hon. Rufus Putnam, June 17, 1783, before the Army disbanded, with a petition signed by 288 officers of the Continental line of the army, which Gen. Washington was asked to bring to the attention of Congress, and urge a speedy redemption of the promises Congress had made the army, he appealed to Congress to take speedy action and provide homes for the soldiers in the Ohio country, where he said, "they may expect after a little perseverance, competence and independence for themselves, a pleasant retreat in old age, and the fairest prospects for their children."

VII. The colonies had become set in their ways. Their people had but little intercourse with each other. Each had its own laws, customs, prejudices, selfish interests, and a people descended from a common stock with peculiarities that distinguished each from the other. The coming storm of revolution, drove them to counsel, common purpose and unity of action. The war of the revolution brought the men from all sections in actual contact with each other. The New England Colonies were settled by the descendants of the Puritans; New York, formerly a Dutch province, was composed of the descendants of the Dutch and English; New Jersey and Pennsylvania were settled by Dutch, Quakers, Germans and English; Maryland was settled by Catholics and loyalists; Virginia and the colonies to its south were settled by cavaliers and loyalists, and by people who were deported for various offenses against English law. These elements are turned toward "Ohio." The sons of the revolution, from Massachusetts, Rhode Island, New Hampshire, and Connecticut, settled on the Ohio Company's purchase at Marietta, and later, in the counties comprising Connecticut's Western Reserve, along the shores of Lake Erie; the soldiers from Virginia found homes in the rich rolling lands of the Scioto Valley, west of the river; the Jersey men followed Symmes to the beautiful valleys of the Little and Big Miami rivers; the German and the Dutch element from the Central States pushed into the central and later the northwest portions of the state. They married and were welded into a happy and harmonious people. A new generation of men were born on the soil of Ohio. The characteristics of the ancestors and of different nationalities disappeared, and were blended into a steady, well bred and well defined man. The native Buckeyes were the first type of American manhood that appeared upon the scene, when "westward the star of empire had arisen."

The Kings of Massachusetts married the Worthingtons of Virginia; the Harrisons of Virginia married the Symmes of New Jersey, and so the hardy pioneers from all the colonies married and intermingled, and the result has been that the first generation born of this happy union has given the state and nation a brainier race of men than has been produced by any state in the Union. It has become a truism in politics, "that the Ohio man wants everything." This is because in the present generation the Ohio man has had all the great important offices, in civil and military life. It was not the result of accident. It was in accordance with the eternal laws of growth and development. It was the result of merit. The Ohio man was the best equipped and best qualified man for the places he was called to fill. In thirty years, we have seen four Ohio born and bred men—Grant, Hayes, Garfield and Harrison fill the office of President. During the civil war, every successful general on the Union side was a Buckeye. Ohio gave to the country such men as Grant, Sherman, Sheridan, McClellan, McDowell, Buell, Rosecrans, Custer, McPherson, Cox, Hayes, the McCooks, (father and sons, four); and many others by adoption and birth. Ohio's sons have filled the following places: Secretary of the Treasury: Ewing, Corwin, Chase, Sherman, Windom and Foster; Secretary of War: Grant, Sherman, Taft and Stanton; Secretary of the Interior: Ewing, Cox and Delano; Attorney General: Stanberry, Taft, Stanton and Harrison; Postmaster General: Meigs, McLean and Dennison; Chief Justices: Chase, Waite and Matthews; Associate Justices: McLean, Swayne and Woods. Beside these who have held offices, there are half a million living in the state who are equally as willing to accept office and fully as capable of filling them.

Rufus King, whose father was a revolutionary soldier from Massachusetts and whose mother was a Worthington from Virginia, says: "No state presented a stronger array of able men, no better proof could be added of the worth of the pioneer stock of Ohio, than that so many of their sons pass to leadership in the greatest crisis of the country's history. It is proof, not only of inherited qualities, but of conscientious family training, the best characteristic of the Anglo-

Saxon race. These distinguished leaders were exponents of a people of like character and training, who gave them prominence and sustained them by suffrage and sacrifice. In the unnamed hosts, incapable of being singled out because of their numbers, there were also heroes and leaders. They it was who filled the ranks of the army and kept their state a creditor, and never a debtor upon any demand for men. It was they who moved in continuous column to the front until the rebellion was suppressed. They were called upon for 306,322 men; they responded with 319,659 soldiers and furnished more than a tenth of the entire army that vindicated the national power, and thus repaid with interest the debt of gratitude, to the authors of the Ordinance of 1787, and the founders of the new state in the "back country," and most gloriously indicated the wisdom and foresight of George Washington, in urging his companions in arms to seek homes in the Ohio Valley. These men and the people of Ohio, are the children of the pioneers from New England and the Middle States and "people to the southward." The Ohio man is not an accident. It is not alone in public offices he has achieved distinction and place. His energies are not solely bent in the pursuit of office. In whatever branch of activity his mental powers are turned, he finds a place in the front ranks and does not rest content in any other. Edison, the wizard of the age, is an Ohio man. The tide of our surplus population is flowing eastward and westward, and under the law of compensation, is giving renewed life to the stock from whence they sprang. The mayor of New York City is an Ohio man. Every leading newspaper in New York City is owned or edited by an Ohio man. The two leading cartoon papers, *Judge* and *Puck*, were founded by Ohio's sons, Keppler and Wales, one from Ashtabula and the other from Sandusky County. Whitelaw Reed, editor and owner of the *Tribune*, was born in Greene County. Col. Wm. Brown, editor and owner of the *News*; Murat Halstead, Jno. R. McLean, of the *Journal*, and other sons of Ohio, are illustrious and occupy the front rank in the Journalism of the Metropolis of the Western Hemisphere.

In law and medicine Ohio's sons now hold prominent places in New York City, as well as in commercial life, and she has turned such gifted men as Samuel Thomas and Calvin S. Brice, loose upon the lambs that stand ready to be fleeced in Wall Street. But here we pause. It is not our mission to extol the great and good whose lives and deeds have made our beloved state so glorious. It is our painful duty to deal with those men and those deeds, that have brought shame to replace honor around the name of Ohio.

VIII. Until 1887, Ohio was an "October" state. Under the first and second Constitutions, the election for state officers took place in October, while the Federal elections were held in November. This required two elections to be held, in October and November, in Presidential years. After the war, when the passions aroused by civil conflict began to cool, parties were more equally divided and Ohio became debatable ground. Here temptation and opportunity presented itself for the use of money to maintain party supremacy. We present from official sources the vote cast at every election since Ohio was admitted to the Union.

VOTE CAST FOR PRESIDENT, GOVERNOR AND SECRETARY OF STATE* AT THE PRESIDENTIAL AND STATE ELECTIONS FROM 1803 TO 1894, INCLUSIVE.

Year.	Office.	Names of Candidates.	Politics.	Number of votes each received.	Total vote cast.
1803	Governor......	Edward Tiffin.........	Republican....	4,564	4,564
1804†	President......	Thomas Jefferson.....	Republican....	2,593	
		Charles C. Pinckney..	Federalist.....	364	
			Scattering.....	256	3,213
1805	Governor......	Edward Tiffin.........	Republican....	4,788	4,788
1807	Governor......	Return J. Meigs, Jr...	Federalist.....	5,550	
		Nathaniel Massie.....	Republican....	4,757	10,307
1808	President......	James Madison	Republican....	No Returns.	
		Charles C. Pinckney..	Federalist.....		
		George Clinton..	Republican....		
1808	Governor......	Samuel Huntington...	Republican....	7,293	
		Thomas Worthington.	Republican....	5,601	
		Thomas Kirker.......	Republican....	3,397	16,291
1810	Governor......	Return J. Meigs, Jr...	Republican....	9,924	
		Thomas Worthington.	Republican....	7,731	17,655
1812	President......	James Madison	Republican....	7,420	
		DeWitt Clinton.......	Federalist.....	3,301	10,721

* From 1803 to 1850 the Secretary of State was elected by the General Assembly.

† The Democratic party of to-day claims lineal descent from the first Republican party with President Jefferson as its founder. Authorities differ as to the date when the party dropped the name Republican and assumed that of Democrat, it being ascribed to various dates between 1805 and 1820.

VOTE CAST AT PRESIDENTIAL AND STATE ELECTIONS, ETC.—*Continued.*

Year.	Office.	Names of Candidates.	Politics.	Number of votes each received.	Total vote cast.
1812	Governor......	Return J. Meigs, Jr...	Federalist.....	11,859	
		Thomas Scott.........	Republican....	7,903	19,762
1814	Governor......	Thomas Worthington.	Republican....	15,879	
		Othniel Looker	Federalist.....	6,171	22,050
1816	President......	James Monroe........	Republican....	3,326	
		Rufus King...........	Federalist.....	593	3,919
1816	Governor......	Thomas Worthington.	Republican....	22,931	
		James Dunlap	Republican....	6,295	
		Ethan A. Brown......	Federalist.....	1,607	30,833
1818	Governor......	Ethan A. Brown......	Republican....	30,194	
		James Dunlap	Republican....	8,075	38,269
1820‡	President	James Monroe........	Democrat......	7,164	
		John Q. Adams.......	Opposition	2,215	9,379
1820	Governor......	Ethan A. Brown......	Democrat	34,836	
		Jeremiah Morrow.....	Democrat	9,426	
		William H. Harrison..	Democrat	4,348	
		Scattering............	....	250	48,860
1822	Governor	Jeremiah Morrow.....	Democrat	26,059	
		Allen Trimble.........	Federalist.....	22,889	
		William W. Irvin	Democrat	11,060	60,008
1824	President......	Andrew Jackson......	Democrat	18,489	
		John Q. Adams.......	Coalition	12,280	
		Wm. H. Crawford	Democrat	....	
		Henry Clay..........	Democrat	19,255	50,024
1824	Governor......	Jeremiah Morrow.....	Democrat	39,526	
		Allen Trimble.........	Nat. Republc'n	37,108	76,634
1826	Governor......	Allen Trimble	Nat. Republc'n	71,475	
		John Bigger	Democrat	4,114	
		Alex. Campbell.......	Republican....	4,765	
		Benjamin Tappan.....	....	4,192	
		Scattering............	....	187	84,733
1828	President......	Andrew Jackson......	Democrat	67,597	
		John Q. Adams.......	Nat. Republc'n	63,396	130,993
1828	Governor......	Allen Trimble.........	Nat. Republc'n	53,971	
		John W. Campbell....	Democrat	51,951	
		Scattering............	....	112	106,034

‡ Political parties were disorganized at the time of the election of John Q. Adams. He claimed to be a Republican as Jefferson, but his doctrines were decidedly federalistic. The opposition to his administration took the name of Democrat and elected Jackson President in 1828.

VOTE CAST AT PRESIDENTIAL AND STATE ELECTIONS, ETC.—*Continued.*

Year.	Office.	Names of Candidates.	Politics.	Number of votes each received.	Total vote cast.
1830	Governor......	Duncan McArthur....	Nat. Republc'n	49,668	
		Robert Lucas.........	Democrat.....	49,186	
		Scattering...........	....	226	99,080
1832	President......	Andrew Jackson	Democrat.....	81,246	
		Henry Clay...........	Nat. Republc'n	76,539	
		William Wirt..........	Anti-Mason...	509	
		John Floyd	Nullifier.......	....	158,294
1832	Governor......	Robert Lucas.........	Democrat.....	71,251	
		Darius Lyman........	Whig..........	63,185	
		Scattering	....	33	134,469
1834	Governor......	Robert Lucas.........	Democrat.....	70,738	
		James Findlay........	Whig..........	67,414	
		Scattering............	....	38	138,190
1836	President......	Martin Van Buren....	Democrat.....	96,238	
		Wm. H. Harrison.....	Whig..........	104,958	
		H. L. White..........	....	....	
		Daniel Webster	....	....	
		W. P. Mangum	....	....	201,196
1836	Governor......	Joseph Vance.........	Whig..........	92,204	
		Eli Baldwin.....	Democrat.....	86,158	
		Scattering............	....	200	178,562
1838	Governor	Wilson Shannon	Democrat.....	107,884	
		Joseph Vance.........	Whig..........	102,146	
		Scattering	....	7	210,037
1840	President......	Wm. H. Harrison.....	Whig..........	148,157	
		Martin Van Buren....	Democrat.....	124,782	
		James G. Birney......	Liberty	903	273,842
1840	Governor......	Thomas Corwin.......	Whig..........	145,442	
		Wilson Shannon	Democrat.....	129,312	
		Scattering	....	8	274,762
1842	Governor......	William Shannon......	Democrat.....	119,774	
		Thomas Corwin.......	Whig..........	117,902	
		Leicester King........	Abolitionist....	5,134	
		Scattering............	....	40	242,850
1844	President......	James K. Polk........	Democrat.....	149,061	
		Henry Clay...........	Whig..........	155,113	
		James G. Birney......	Liberty	8,050	312,224
1844	Governor	Mordecai Bartley.....	Whig..........	146,333	
		David Todd...........	Democrat.....	145,062	
		Leicester King........	Abolitionist....	8,898	
		Scattering............	....	11	300,304

VOTE CAST AT PRESIDENTIAL AND STATE ELECTIONS, ETC.—*Continued.*

Year.	Office.	Names of Candidates.	Politics.	Number of votes each received.	Total vote cast.
1846	Governor	William Bebb	Whig	118,869	
		David Todd	Democrat	116,484	
		Samuel Lewis	Abolitionist	10,797	
		Scattering		46	246,196
1848	President	Zachary Taylor	Whig	138,359	
		Lewis Cass	Democrat	154,773	
		Martin Van Buren	Free Soil	35,347	328,479
1848	Governor	Seabury Ford	Whig	148,756	
		John B. Weller	Democrat	148,445	
		Scattering		742	297,943
1850	Governor	Reuben Wood	Democrat	133,093	
		William Johnson	Whig	121,105	
		Edward Smith	Abolitionist	13,747	267,945
1851	Governor	Reuben Wood	Democrat	145,654	
		Samuel F. Vinton	Whig	119,548	
		Samuel Lewis	Abolitionist	10,918	
		Scattering		62	282,182
1851	Sec'y of State	Wm. Trevitt	Democrat	145,686	
		Earl Bill	Whig	120,256	
		Henry W. King	Free Soil	15,768	281,660
1852	President	Franklin Pierce	Democrat	168,933	
		Winfield Scott	Whig	152,523	
		John P. Hale	Free Soil	31,732	353,188
1853	Governor	William Medill	Democrat	147,663	
		Nelson Barrere	Whig	85,857	
		Samuel Lewis	Abolitionist	50,346	283,866
1853	Sec'y of State	Wm. Trevitt	Democrat	151,818	
		Nelson Van Vorhes	Whig	97,500	
		William Graham	Free Soil	33,518	
		Scattering		409	283,245
1855	Governor	Salmon P. Chase	Republican	146,770	
		William Medill	Democrat	131,019	
		Allen Trimble	American	24,276	302,065
1855	Sec'y of State	James H. Baker	Rep. and Am.	168,724	
		William Trevitt	Democrat	133,641	302,365
1856	President	James Buchanan	Democrat	170,874	
		John C. Fremont	Republican	187,497	
		Millard Fillmore	American	28,126	386,497
1857	Governor	Salmon P. Chase	Republican	160,568	
		H. B. Payne	Democrat	159,065	
		P. Van Trump	American	10,272	329,905

VOTE CAST AT PRESIDENTIAL AND STATE ELECTIONS, ETC.—*Continued.*

Year.	Office.	Names of Candidates.	Politics.	Number of votes each received.	Total vote cast.
1857	Sec'y of State..	Addison P. Russell ...	Republican....	161,837	
		Jacob Reinhard.......	Democrat	159,421	
		C. C. Allen	American	10,381	
		Scattering	....	278	331,917
1859	Governor......	William Dennison.....	Republican....	184,557	
		Rufus P. Ranney.....	Democrat	171,226	355,733
1859	Sec'y of State..	Addison P. Russell ...	Republican....	184,839	
		Jacob Reinhard.......	Democrat	170,400	355,239
1860	President......	Abraham Lincoln.....	Republican	221,809	
		Stephen A. Douglas ..	Ind. Democrat	187,421	
		John Bell.	Const. Union..	12,193	
		John C. Breckinridge.	Democrat	11,303	
		Gerritt Smith.........	Abolitionist....	136	432,862
1861	Governor......	David Todd	Republican....	206,997	
		Hugh J. Jewett	Democrat......	151,774	
		Scattering	....	109	358,830
1861	Sec'y of State..	Benj. R. Cowan.	Republican....	207,352	
		William W. Armstrong	Democrat	151,912	
		Scattering	....	181	359,445
1862	Sec'y of State..	William W. Armstrong	Democrat	184,315	
		Wilson S. Kennon.....	Republican....	178,755	363,070
1863	Governor......	John Brough..........	Republican....	288,826	
		C. L. Vallandigham...	Democrat	187,728	476,554
1864	President......	Abraham Lincoln.....	Republican....	265,654	
		George B. McClellan..	Democrat	205,599	471,253
1864	Sec'y of State..	William Henry Smith.	Republican....	238,145	
		William W. Armstrong	Democrat	183,842	421,987
1865	Governor......	Jacob D. Cox.........	Republican....	223,642	
		George W. Morgan...	Democrat. ...	193,797	
		Scattering	....	360	417,799
1866	Sec'y of State..	Willaim Henry Smith.	Republican....	256,302	
		Benjamin LeFever....	Democrat	213,606	469,903
1867	Governor......	R. B. Hayes...... ...	Republican....	243,605	
		A. G. Thurman.......	Democrat	240,622	484,227
1868	President......	U. S. Grant..........	Republican....	280,167	
		Horatio Seymour......	Democrat	238,621	518,783
1868	Sec y of State..	Isaac R. Sherwood....	Republican....	267,066	
		Thos. Hubbard.......	Democrat	249,682	516,748

VOTE CAST AT PRESIDENTIAL AND STATE ELECTIONS, ETC.—*Continued.*

Year.	Office.	Names of Candidates.	Politics.	Number of votes each received.	Total vote cast.
1869	Governor......	R. B. Hayes	Republican....	236,082	
		G. H. Pendleton......	Democrat	228,576	
		Samuel Scott..........	Prohibition....	679	
					465,337
1870	Sec'y of State..	Isaac R. Sherwood....	Republican....	221,708	
		William Heisley.......	Democrat	205,018	
		Jay Odell............	Prohibition....	2,833	
					429,559
1871	Governor......	Edward F. Noyes.....	Republican....	238,273	
		George W. McCook ..	Democrat	218,105	
		Gideon T. Stewart....	Prohibition....	4,068	
					460,446
1872	President......	U. S. Grant...........	Republican....	281,852	
		Horace Greeley.......	Dem. and Lib.	244,321	
		James Black..........	Temperance...	2,100	
		Charles O'Conor......	Democrat	1,163	
		Scattering	....	162	
					529,598
1872	Sec'y of State .	Allen T. Wikoff.......	Republican....	265,925	
		Aquila Wiley	Democrat	251,778	
		F. Schumacher	Prohibition....	2,035	
					519,733
1873	Governor......	Edward F. Noyes.....	Republican....	213,837	
		William Allen.........	Democrat	214,654	
		Gideon T. Stewart....	Prohibition....	10,278	
		Isaac C. Collins.......	....	10,109	
					448,878
1874	Sec'y of State..	Allen T. Wikoff.......	Republican....	221,204	
		William Bell, Jr.......	Democrat	238,406	
		John R. Buchtel......	Prohibition....	7,815	
					467,425
1875	Governor......	R. B. Hayes..........	Republican....	297,817	
		William Allen.........	Democrat......	292,273	
		Jay Odell............	Prohibition....	2,593	
		Scattering	....	17	
					592,700
1876	President......	R. B. Hayes..........	Republican....	330,698	
		Samuel J. Tilden......	Democrat	323,182	
		G. Clay Smith........	Prohibition....	1,636	
		Peter Cooper..........	Greenback.....	3,057	
		Scattering	....	1,198	
					659,771
1876	Sec'y of State..	Milton Barnes.........	Republican....	317,856	
		William Bell, Jr.......	Democrat	311,220	
		E. S. Chapman........	Prohibition....	1,863	
					630,939
1877	Governor......	William H. West......	Republican....	249,105	
		Richard M. Bishop ...	Democrat	271,625	
		Lewis H. Bond	....	12,489	
		Stephen Johnson......	....	16,912	
		Henry A. Thompson..	Prohibition....	4,836	
					554,967

VOTE CAST AT PRESIDENTIAL AND STATE ELECTIONS, ETC.—*Continued.*

Year.	Office.	Names of Candidates.	Politics.	Number of votes each received.	Total vote cast.
1878	Sec'y of State..	Milton Barnes.........	Republican....	274,120	
		David R. Paige.......	Democrat	270,966	
		Andrew Roy..........	Greenback	38,332	
		Jeremiah N. Robinson	Prohibition....	5,682	589,100
1879	Governor......	Charles Foster........	Republican....	336,261	
		Thomas Ewing........	Democrat	319,132	
		Gideon T. Stewart....	Prohibition....	4,145	
		A. Sanders Piatt......	Greenback	9,072	
		John Hood...........	....	547	669,157
1880	President......	James A. Garfield.....	Republican....	375,048	
		Winfield S. Hancock..	Democrat	340,821	
		James B. Weaver.....	Greenback	6,456	
		Neal Dow............	Prohibition....	2,616	
		Scattering	....	26	724,967
1880	Sec'y of State..	Charles Townsend ...	Republican....	362,021	
		William Lang.........	Democrat	343,016	
		Charles A. Lloyd.....	Greenback	6,786	
		William H. Doane	Prohibition....	2,815	
		Scattering	....	1,548	716,186
1881	Governor......	Charles Foster........	Republican....	312,735	
		John W. Bookwalter..	Democrat	288,426	
		Abraham R. Ludlow..	Prohibition....	16,597	
		John Seitz...........	Greenback	6,630	
		Scattering	....	138	624,226
1882	Sec'y of State..	Chas. Townsend......	Republican....	297,759	
		James W. Newman...	Democrat	316,874	
		F. Schumacher........	Prohibition....	12,202	
		George L. Hafer......	Greenback.....	5,345	
		Scattering	....	2,915	635,095
1883	Governor	Joseph B. Foraker....	Republican....	347,164	
		George Hoadly.......	Democrat	359,693	
		F. Schnmacher	Prohibition....	8,362	
		Charles Jenkins.......	Greenback	2,937	
		Scattering	....	3,154	721,310
1884	President......	James G. Blaine.......	Republican....	400,082	
		Grover Cleveland.....	Democrat	368,280	
		John P. St. John......	Prohibition....	11,069	
		Benj. F. Butler........	Union Labor..	5,179	
		Scattering	....	2,549	787,159
1884	Sec'y of State..	James S. Robinson....	Republican....	391,597	
		James W. Newman...	Democrat	380,355	
		Peter M. Harold......	Union Labor..	3,475	
		Evan J. Morris........	Prohibition....	8,007	
		Scattering	....	1,657	785,691

Vote Cast at Presidential and State Elections, etc.—*Continued.*

Year.	Office.	Names of Candidates.	Politics.	Number of votes each received.	Total vote cast.
1885	Governor......	Joseph B. Foraker....	Republican....	359,281	
		George Hoadly	Democrat......	341,830	
		Adna B. Leonard	Prohibition....	28,081	
		John W. Northrop....	Greenback....	2,001	
		Scattering	....	2,774	733,967
1886	Sec'y of State..	James S. Robinson....	Republican....	341,095	
		John McBride	Democrat	329,314	
		Henry K. Smith	Prohibition....	28,982	
		Charles Bonsall.......	Greenback....	2,010	
		Scattering............	....	2,832	704,233
1887	Governor......	Joseph B. Foraker....	Republican....	356,534	
		Thomas E. Powell	Democrat......	333,205	
		John Seitz	Union Labor..	24,711	
		Morris Sharp.........	Prohibition....	29,700	
		Scattering	....	2,820	746,970
1888	President......	Benjamin Harrison....	Republican....	416,054	
		Grover Cleveland.....	Democrat	396,455	
		Clinton B. Fiske......	Prohibition....	24,356	
		Alson J. Streeter......	Union Labor..	3,496	
		Scattering.	....	1,580	844,941
1888	Sec'y of State..	Daniel J. Ryan	Republican	416,510	
		Boston G. Young	Democrat	395,522	
		Walter S. Payne......	Prohibition....	24,618	
		George F. Ebner......	Union Labor..	3,452	
		Scattering	....	1,839	841,941
1889	Governor......	Joseph B. Foraker....	Republican....	368,551	
		James E. Campbell....	Democrat	379,423	
		John B. Helwig.......	Prohibition....	26,504	
		John H. Rhoads	Union Labor..	1,048	
		Scattering	....	195	775,721
1890	Sec'y of State..	Daniel J. Ryan.......	Republican....	363,548	
		Thaddeus E. Cromley	Democrat	352,579	
		Mel'thon C. Lockwood	Prohibition....	23,837	
		Ezekiel T. Curtis	Union Labor..	1,752	
		Scattering	....	470	742,186
1891	Governor......	William McKinley, Jr.	Republican....	386,739	
		James E. Campbell....	Democrat	365,228	
		John J. Ashenhurst...	Prohibition....	20,190	
		John Seitz	Peoples........	23,472	
		Scattering	....	2	795,631
1892	President	Benjamin Harrison ...	Republican....	405,187	
		Grover Cleveland....	Democrat	404,115	
		James B. Weaver	Peoples........	14,850	
		John Bidwell.........	Prohibition....	26,012	
		Scattering	....	11,461	861,625

VOTE CAST AT PRESIDENTIAL AND STATE ELECTIONS, ETC.—*Concluded.*

Year.	Office.	Names of Candidates.	Politics.	Number of votes each received.	Total vote cast.
1892	Sec'y of State..	Samuel M. Taylor	Republican....	402,540	
		William A. Taylor....	Democrat.....	401,451	
		Solon C. Thayer......	Peoples.......	14,554	
		George L. Case.......	Prohibition....	25,885	
		Scattering	....	11,946	
					861,625
1893	Governor......	William McKinley...	Republican....	433,342	
		Lawrence T. Neal	Democrat	352,347	
		Gideon P. Macklin....	Prohibition....	22,406	
		Edward J. Bracken...	Peoples........	15,563	
					835,604
1894	Sec'y of State..	Samuel M. Taylor.....	Republican....	413,989	
		Milton Turner........	Democrat	276,902	
		Mark G. McCaslin....	Prohibition...	23,237	
		Charles R. Martin....	Peoples........	49,495	
		Scattering	....	1	
					776,819

The Democrats and Jeffersonian Republicans have carried the state 34 times; the Whigs 8 times, and the Republicans, under various names and alliances, 51 times. The plurality has been small, often being less than 5000. The first appearance of the use of money to effect results by influencing people corruptly, was with the advent of Charles Foster, of Fostoria, O., as a candidate for Congress in '70, '72, 74, '76 and '78. He lived in the town in which he was born. He was a man of affairs. He was engaged in mercantile pursuits and profited by the opportunities presented by the war. He accumulated a fortune and branched out into investments in manufactures and railroad improvements. He built up Fostoria, which was named by his father, and made a thriving town of it. He was a man of pleasant address, sound judgment, and good sense. He was friendly to all who knew him, was easy of approach, and popular among his neighbors. In looking about for other worlds to conquer his restless genius led him into the field of politics. He was nominated for Congress. The district was Democratic. He introduced business methods into his campaigns. He did not trust to noise and excitement. He perfected the party organization; a thorough poll was made. This enabled him to form an accurate estimate of the number of votes he needed. Knowing this, the places were found, the prices were ascertained, and the money was placed in proper hands the night before the election, and such voters as could be reached by money were "fixed." Chas. Foster was elected several times by a small majority in a Democratic district. His phenomenal success was attributed to his great popularity. It was due chiefly to his use of money. In 1879 he was nominated for Governor, at Cincinnati. Judge Taft was the choice of his party, but Chas. Foster was declared the nominee. He owed his nomination to money. He was elected Governor twice. His ambition grew with his success. He was a candidate for Senator, but had to give way to others. Ohio had too many great men. They were crowding each other. Garfield and Sherman were ahead of Foster in the class of promotion, and he had to wait. While he was waiting his expenses continued. He was appointed Secretary of the Treasury, to fill the vacancy occasioned by the death of Mr. Windom. He retired in 1893. His devotion to politics had ruined his business. He became a bankrupt. His splendid fortune had been dissipated in politics. Many who trusted him absolutely have lost their homes and faith in humanity. Chas. Foster will never recover. His wreck — his fortune gone and a good name lost, teach a solemn and impressive lesson. His code of morals was a dangerous and a desperate one. In politics, he believed that his party was always right, and the Democratic party was always wrong, and any act was justifiable that would defeat his political opponents. Upon this specious theory he soothed his conscience; used his money to corrupt the people; committed a crime to do good, and justified his acts by the success of his party and the achievement of his personal ambition. He was the pioneer and apostle of Boodle in Ohio. He was the first to introduce a system that has brought disgrace upon the name of Ohio. His acts can never be undone. Their influence for evil can never be estimated. There is no punishment to fit his crime. He will leave nothing but a ruined reputation and an apt pupil in the person of Calvin S. Brice, who has taken up the work where Chas. Foster left it off, and has already added to the shame of his native state by the unblushing infamy of his acts and methods. The example of Chas. Foster, wrecked, ruined and disgraced, seems to have no deterring effect. Similar acts must lead to similar results. The eternal laws of justice are equal in their operation and the results in Calvin S. Brice's case must be the same.

"Aye, Justice, who evades her?
  Her scales reach every heart;
The action and the motive
  She weigheth each apart;
And none who swerve from right or truth
  Can 'scape her penalty."

— *Hall's Poems.*

MILKING THE SPRINGFIELD HEIFER.

(*Porcupine, Jan. 1890.*)

CHAPTER V.

APPROACHING THE RAPIDS.

A GOOD government, well administered, is the first blessing to a people. Everything desirable in life is thereby secured to them; and from the operation of wholesome and equal laws, the passions of men are restrained within due bounds; their actions receive a proper direction; the virtues are cultivated, and the healthful fabric of civilized life is reared and brought to perfection.

* * * * * * * * * *

"But with all the care and attention to your interest and happiness that can be taken, you have many difficulties to struggle with. The subduing a new country, notwithstanding its natural advantages, is alone an arduous task; a task, however, that patience and perseverance will surmount. And these virtues, so necessary in every situation, but particularly so in yours, you must resolve to exercise. Neither is the reducing a country from the state of nature to a state of cultivation so irksome, as from a slight or superficial view may appear. Even very sensible pleasures attend it. The gradual progress of improvement fills the mind with delectable ideas. Vast forests converted into arable fields, and cities rising in places which were lately the habitation of wild beasts, give a pleasure something like that attendant on creation, if we can form an idea of it. The imagination is ravished, and a taste communicated of the joy of God to see a 'happy world.'

"The advantages, however, are not merely imaginary. Situated as you are, in the most temperate climate; favored with the most fertile soil; surrounded by the noblest and most beautiful rivers; every portion of labor will meet its due reward. But you have upon your frontier numbers of savages, and, too often, hostile nations. Against them it is necessary that you should be guarded.

* * * * * * * * * *

"Run not into their customs and habits, which is but too frequent with those who settle near them; but endeavor to induce them to adopt yours. Prevent by every means that dreadful reproach, perhaps too justly brought by them against all the white people they have yet been acquainted with, that, professing the most holy and benevolent religion, they are uninfluenced by its dictates and regardless of its people."
—*Extracts from the inaugural address of Gov. Arthur St. Clair, Marietta, O., July 18, 1788.*

A century has passed since the first governor of Ohio and the Northwestern Territory delivered his address to a handful of men, women and children, less than 200, on the edge of a vast wilderness. Five states and part of a sixth have arisen in that territory. Over twelve millions of people now live in that country. The vast forests have been converted into arable fields. Cities have arisen in number and importance beyond the conceptions of the wildest enthusiast. The savage so dreaded has disappeared forever, and in his place have come other foes, more dangerous to our civilization, our homes, and our institutions than the untutored red man. The Indian, justly enraged by the encroachments of the whites, saw the graves of his ancestors disturbed; the game driven off; the forests destroyed; his fields and towns ruined; himself and his family menaced amidst the hills and valleys, where they were born, and by a people who proclaimed a new God of peace. They saw the white man come with the gospel of love in one hand, and a rifle in the other, and as he lifted his voice in prayer to the mysterious being, he never took his eye off of the rifle-sight. These contradictions, and the outrages of many years, made the Indian doubt the professions of the white man. Being a human being he naturally retaliated. He killed, scalped, captured, tortured and destroyed, but in vain. The tide was resistless. But while he tortured and destroyed the bodies of our pioneer fathers, he never assailed their reputations. He spared their good names. In our modern politics we have savages that excel in brutality the most atrocious deeds of the relentless Indians. Good name, character, home, and its loved ones are not saved from the destruction and assaults of our modern political warfare. It is a merciless conflict, in which only a few of the fittest ever survive.

II. Lincoln died April 15, 1865, the first presidential victim in a free country, to a maddened and blinded politician's rage. His death was a public calamity. But as subsequent events have proven, it was fortunate for his own fame, that he died when he did. He lived to see victory crown the efforts of our armies. The war was over. The Union was preserved. The difficulties that confronted the government were greater than those conquered in the civil war. In carrying out his ideas of the treatment that should be accorded the seceding states, the rebel and the negro, it is doubtful if Mr. Lincoln would not have entered upon a contest that would have alienated a great portion of his party following, and aroused the antipathy of the people of the North. He had borne enough. Providence had provided a great character to guide the destinies of a distracted people in the dark hours of a civil war. He had done his work successfully. The bells had not ceased their joyous clamor over the final triumph, when that shot rang out that terminated the life of this great man. His fame is secured. His virtues, his genius, his words, his deeds will become brighter as the years cycle into centuries and ages; and minds yet unborn, will never grow weary in studying the achievements and sounding the praises of this grandest character of the nineteenth, if not of all the centuries. Even in the South, before the generation of those who struggled so heroically for a lost cause, the "bloody and vulgar tyrant, Abe Lincoln," has been acknowledged and is revered as "a noble and benevolent instrument, sent by Providence to save a people." The reconstruction of the states lately in rebellion, and the treatment of rebel and slave, were the great problems that occupied the public mind after the war, and aroused public feeling, and at times the latter was more bitter and the lines more fiercely and closely drawn than during the war. President Johnson's uncertain policy and vacillating conduct enraged the partisans who had made him Vice-President. War and its conditions drove many men of conflicting views into political association, in what was known as the Republican party. The preservation of the Union was the only bond that held them together. Whigs, Abolitionists, Knownothings, Free Soilers, Anti-slavery Democrats, all flocked into the ark of Republicanism, pending the storm.

When it was over their former prejudices and principles began to assert themselves, and like the animal under similar circumstances, there was a tendency to return to their former state. Andrew Johnson was born and reared a Democrat, and when he became President and his highest ambitions had been realized, there was no longer reason to deceive himself and others, and his early training asserted itself. A man may join another party, but he cannot change the convictions of a lifetime, however much he may want to or may think he can.

III. During the war, Ohio had, according to James G. Blaine in "His Twenty Years in Congress," a delegation of the ablest men in that body. At the time of Lincoln's death, its character had changed as to men, but had not diminished as to ability and influence. In the Senate she had Sherman and Wade, and in the House were such men as Hayes, Schenck, Le Blond, Lawrence, Shellabarger, Hubbell, Buckland, Ashley, Bundy, Delano, Bingham, Spaulding and Garfield. Two of these afterwards became President, and are dead. Le Blond, Lawrence, Delano, Ashley, Bundy and Bingham are still living, having exceeded the Psalmist's "three score years and ten." In 1864, Salmon P. Chase had desired to succeed Lincoln as President, but the latter having been endorsed almost unanimously by the Ohio Legislature, Chase wisely withdrew and was honored with a place upon the Supreme Bench. In 1864, Lincoln and Johnson were opposed by two sons of Ohio, McClellan and Pendleton, for President and Vice-President, upon a platform which declared that the war was a failure. Fortunately the platform was wrong and the candidates were a failure. Johnson's proposition to make treason odious by wholesale executions and confiscations, did not merit the approval of the popular mind and heart. The men who had done the fighting on both sides had seen enough blood spilt; while only some of those who had helped to put down the rebellion with their mouths, were shouting for more gore as a daily beverage. Benjamin Wade, in consulting with President Johnson, as to his proposed policy of extermination, did not favor a wholesale slaughter. He thought the offering up of ten or dozen would do, and at the extreme he was not willing to sacrifice more than "a baker's dozen," and he thought he could select the victims, so that the choice would be generally satisfactory.

When party lines are so sharply defined, there are no stragglers between the opposing organizations, and there is little opportunity and less need for the corrupt use of money to affect results.

In 1865, Gen. J. D. Cox was the Republican candidate for governor, and Gen. Geo. W. Morgan was the Democratic candidate. 427,430 votes were polled. This was 5,000 votes less than were polled in the Lincoln-Douglas campaign of 1860, and 44,000 votes less than were polled in the Presidential campaign of 1864; Cox polled 233,033 votes and Morgan 193,797, the Republican majority being 39,836. In 1866, the Republicans cast 256,302 votes, and the Democrats 213,606. In 1867, the war amendments were the issue. The doubtful experiment was to be made of admitting the emancipated slave to the body of citizenship, not as a matter of justice or for the public welfare, but as a party necessity. His vote was needed to help maintain the supremacy, not of principles but of a party. Before the war, in the campaign of 1856, between Buchanan and Fremont, we remember our first political contest. It was charged by the Democrats that the new party, the Republicans, were not only opposed to slavery, but were in favor of placing the negro upon equal terms with the whites.

This of course was said to arouse the passions and fears of the more ignorant class of voters. In a procession, a wagon load of young ladies carried a banner, demanding "white husbands or none." Some of them have lived to see the laws repealed that made it illegal to marry a negro.

Gen. R. B. Hayes, of New England stock, was the Republican candidate, and Allen G. Thurman, one of "the people from the Southward," a Virginian by birth, was the Democratic candidate. Both had served in Congress. Lucy Webb, Mr. Hayes' wife, was a native of Chillicothe, Thurman's adopted town. He represented the Ross district in '45 and '46, when the famous Walker tariff law was passed by the Democrats. His uncle, Wm. Allen, was at the same time a member of the Senate. Thurman was elected a judge of the Supreme Court under the new Constitution. He was engaged in the pursuits of peace and practice of his profession, while Hayes was a general in the army. Thurman and Hayes were friends and had long been acquaintances. On their part the canvass was a clean one. While their partisans were bitter and personal, they treated each other as the leader of his party, with decent consideration. Hayes received 243,605 votes, and 240,622 voted for Thurman. Hayes was elected governor, by a majority of 2,983 votes. The Democrats carried the Legislature. Clement L. Vallandingham expected to be chosen United States Senator. He was disappointed. Allen G.

Thurman was elected to succeed Benj. Wade. The Democrats had polled the largest vote they had ever cast in the history of the state. Hayes received 22,000 votes less than had been given Lincoln in 1864, and 45,000 less than had been counted but not cast for Brough in 1863. The strength of the Democrats astonished the Republicans and surprised the whole country. Its only significance was the prejudice against the negro. It remains to be seen whether the Anglo-Saxon, by constitution and laws, can break down the barriers of nature and lift an inferior race to a level which the white man has attained through unnumbered ages of suffering, growth and development, while the black man, as an evidence of the truth of the laws of evolution, halted in the road to civilization amidst environments that solely required him to indulge those appetites and passions, that kept alive the animal, or reproduced his kind.

The chasm between the white man and the black is too wide to be bridged by laws; as Lincoln truthfully said before the war, that "this country could not be part slave and part free; it must be all slave or all free." So the black man will not always be content to serve, and the white man never will permit him to rule. Time and its troubles will make evident the truth or falsity of this proposition, and that at no distant day.

IV. The Ohio man was an important factor in the politics of 1868. Gen. Grant had been nominated for President by the Republicans at Philadelphia. The Democratic convention met in New York City, on the Fourth of July. The Ohio delegation, under the masterful manipulation of Washington McLean, was present with a candidate in the person of Geo. H. Pendleton, "Young Greenbacks," and a platform to make the "greenbacks" a legal tender for all debts. The candidate was beaten, but the platform was adopted, and the "Ohio idea" was born.

In 1862, when the legal tender act was proposed and was pending in Congress, Geo. H. Pendleton was the first to oppose the measure, and point out the evils that had followed in the train of a paper currency, based on nothing but hope and a promise to pay, in the history of every nation that had attempted the experiment. He quoted the words of Daniel Webster, "that gold and silver currency is the law of the land at home, the law of the world abroad, and in the present condition of the world there can be no other currency." But Pendleton, Vallandingham and others, under the influence of Washington McLean, whose earnest advocacy would not be denied, abandoned the teachings of Democracy in favor of "hard money," gold and silver, as provided by the Constitution, and ventured upon dangerous and forbidden paths.

Since 1868, the Democratic party has boxed the compass, and occupied every side, and advocated every possible phase of the money question, except outright repudiation, and now it is about to complete its performances by being misled under the guise of sound money, to repudiate one of the metals expressly provided by the Constitution, and return to a wild cat banking system, as advocated by the national platform of 1892, and approved by Secretary Carlisle in his recent Memphis speech. There should be no mystery about money, in the financial system of a free people. When there is, there is dishonesty and rascality. The present conflict between the standards, gold and silver, is not a skirmish. It is a battle. It should be waged until its conclusion will fix forever the financial system of the United States upon a permanent basis. The student in search of truth can discover that there is an element of right in the contention of both the gold and silver extremists, and the principle of adjustment must be found in a line between the two, but not in a compromise with either.

The framers of the Constitution, suffering from the evils of the worthless Continental currency, took from the states the power to coin money and fix its value, and emit bills of credit, and provided that Congress should have the power to "coin money, regulate the value thereof and of foreign coin," and the states are forbidden to "make anything but gold and silver coin a tender in payment of debts." In regulating the value of coin, Congress had power to fix the ratio of value between gold and silver, but Congress had no power to discriminate against the use of either gold or silver. The same section of the Constitution which authorizes Congress to "coin money and regulate the value thereof," authorizes it "to *fix* the standard of weights and measures." If Congress, having "*fixed*" the length of the yard stick, and the size of the bushel, had proceeded to change and disturb these standards of weight and measures from time to time, confusion would have resulted and faith in them destroyed, and their usefulness would have ended. Congress can "regulate" the "value of gold and silver" as to each other, but having fixed the unit of value and the weight and fineness of gold and silver, it can do no more. Laws and Legislators cannot make values. Labor does that, trade and commerce help. Having deprived the states of the Union of the power to "emit bills of credit," which led to untold evils in the colonies during the revolutionary war, the framers of the Constitution expected Congress to provide a national and uniform system of currency and banking. This, Congress failed to do, and up to the war over slavery, the states were permitted, by sufferance, to do that which the Constitution expressly prohibited, and a "wild cat" system of banking sprang up, with an unlimited system of unsecure and worthless paper money. Certainly the states, being prohibited by the Federal Constitution from making anything a tender in payment of debts "but gold and silver," could not delegate to individuals or corporations a power that they did not possess themselves. Yet this was done for fifty years, and the result was the usual and universal harvest of speculation, panic, disaster, distress. Not only once but repeatedly

Never in the history of the world, had an intelligent and civilized people so persistently closed their eyes to all the impressive lessons of the past, as to financial matters, as did the people of the United States of America, and never did a people pay heavier penalties for outraging the principles that human experience taught were the only safe ones to follow. Perhaps no other government or people could have survived the financial blunders and disasters that mark the history of this country during the first century of its existence. If the American people are to learn nothing from their own immediate past, if the blunders of the past century are to be repeated in the next, it is certain that this experiment of a government, "by the people and for the people," must prove an absolute and dismal failure.

When the temptations of place and power can lead such able, educated, well born and favored men as Geo. H. Pendleton, to abandon the principles of his party and the convictions of a lifetime, it is an evidence of such tremendous forces at work in our boasted civilization, that it raises the doubt, as to whether there be strength enough in our free institutions always to restrain them. There is not a branch of our government, with its nicely adjusted balances and safeguards against the excesses of the popular will, that has not at one time, separately or in unison, bowed to the heresies of the hour, and trampled down the constitutional barriers. Even the Supreme Court, a tribunal that our fathers in their wisdom sought to place above the storms and passions of the people and the hour, has declared the Greenback Act unconstitutional, and then reversed itself, under a pressure of either passion or corruption, or both, that by their decision they made the humiliating confession that they were too weak to resist. The measure which war and its necessities made permissible, has become a menace in peace.

The greenbacks which were to be limited in quantity, and redeemed in something of value, still stand, to the number of 346,000,000 millions, as a monument to party perfidy and human frailty. As the result of the war and its subsequent legislation, we have the most variegated system of currency that the world ever saw, and the colors in Joseph's coat could not outnumber the different degrees, and grades, and kinds of money. We have bonds, bearing various rates of interest; we have copper, nickel, silver in small coins, silver dollars, gold, national bank notes, silver certificates, treasury notes, gold certificates and silver bullion; some a lawful tender for "all debts, public and private," and some payable in gold, some in silver and some in both. It is this system that some parties wish to continue, and others wish to make worse.

This government must have a uniform currency, payable to all persons, for all purposes, and based on something of absolute value. The constitution says, that gold and silver shall constitute this value, and the Supreme Court says, a paper currency may be issued by the government in time of peace. There should be a dollar's worth of gold and silver in the vaults of the National Treasury at all times for every paper dollar issued. Gold and silver are too valuable to be placed in actual use. All governments refuse to receive their own coins when slightly worn, or disfigured, or clipped. There is not gold and silver enough in the world to transact its business. There never will be. It will grow less in proportion to population each year. All the gold and silver in the world used for money, is estimated in round numbers at 8,000 millions, about equally divided between the two metals. If gathered together it would occupy less space than Bunker Hill monument, which is 30 feet square at the base, and 221 feet high, occupying about 150,000 cubic feet. Four nations, England, France, Germany and Russia, have nearly all the gold in the world, and control its financial affairs. The United States is a province of England; she pays more tribute every year to the people opposed to her commercial supremacy, in interest on bonds, than the revenues of the Roman Empire amounted to in the height of her power. No other government could long survive the drain that America is subjected to. America cannot stand it long.

We must have a financial system that will compel those we owe to take our surplus products and not our gold to pay interest. The government should place a popular loan upon the market, to be taken by our people, in bonds of a small denomination, at a low rate of interest, and running for one hundred years. This should be used to accumulate 1,000 millions, if needed, in gold and silver, to become the basis of a national and uniform currency. Money orders in any sum, at low rates, should be issued through the postal department. A system of postal deposits, also should be provided for, where any sums could be deposited and draw a low rate of interest, for stated periods. Any holder of gold or silver bullion, in quantities worth a thousand dollars or more, should be allowed to deposit the same at any government mint, and receive a certificate stating the amount and fineness of the same, and leave the market to do what it does now: fix its value. These certificates should draw no rate of interest, but should be used by all banks as the basis for any circulating medium that they might desire to be issued by the government. The government would hold the actual gold and silver, that would guarantee the safety of every dollar. Experience has amply demonstrated, that banks cannot be trusted with the gold and silver, to redeem circulation.

No gold or silver should be coined as money, and if kept in bulk, very little would be shipped either at home or abroad. The certificates would answer for large commercial transactions. There would be no idle capital. If money could not find use in manufacturing and business, it could be deposited with the government at a low rate of interest, and would only remain there until it could find more profitable employment in business. The currency should be fixed at a stated amount per capita after each Federal census, and there should be a stated increase each year to meet the growth of population and business. This would give stability and prevent speculation and uncertainty. Bankers object to this. They want to transact the money business of the country. They want the government to go out of the banking business. It is not the business of a banker to make or issue money. Experience has proven that it would be both criminal and calamitous to entrust this sovereign power to individuals or corporations. A banker is a money loaner. The three golden balls were hung first over the doors of the early bankers. They belong there now. The banker is not a philanthropist. He does not open his bank with daily prayer, and close it with a benediction. He prospers by the needs and distresses of others. He is the Shylock always standing at the altar of gain, with his knife whetted and crying for "justice and his pound of flesh." Bankers are not worse than other men, but the opportunities and temptations of their business are too strong for poor, weak humanity to resist. There are more laws upon our statute books to regulate the uses and punish the abuses of money in the banking business, than there are to punish or prevent any branch of crime.

The banker is not a patriot. He has no claims upon a nation's gratitude. Money is cowardly. It always hides when there is danger. In the midst of civil strife, when our national existence was threatened, he stood like a highwayman, with his gun at the head of the nation, and made it stand and deliver on his terms. He dictated our financial legislation in the dark hours of the war, by taking advantage of our distresses. He has controlled the legislation since the war by questionable methods. The banker as a class is not a safe counselor or disinterested party in shaping legislation for a free people. Let our statesmen follow the path made plain by the Constitution and by experience. Let them give us a national system of currency, based on actual values. Let us lead the nations of the world. Let us do it now, before our country is burdened with a vast population that the earth cannot feed, and our laws will not control.

VII. Such men as Allen G. Thurman, C. L. Vallandingham, Geo. E. Pugh and Geo. W. Morgan, appeared in the Ohio delegation at the National Convention. Under the powerful influence and personal magnetism of Washington McLean, nearly all but Allen G. Thurman were bitten and badly poisoned by the Greenback snake. The "Confederate Brigadier" made his reappearance in politics and the counsels of the Democratic party. He was busy four years before trying to prove that the declaration that the war was a failure, was true, and having escaped the perils of war and Andrew Johnson's wrath, he cared little what the platform contained, so that it (the platform) declared against the reconstruction legislation that followed the war. This was done. Mr. Johnson wanted to be nominated for the Presidency by a party that he had bitterly opposed, and was ready to denounce and oppose the party that had elected him to the second place four years before. S. P. Chase was a candidate. In the fight for the Senatorship, in the Ohio legislature, a few months before, Pendleton and his friends had aided Thurman to secure the caucus nomination over Vallandingham. The latter never recovered from this defeat. He felt that he was justly entitled to the place by reason of his services, and by virtual promises made during the campaign, which were both explicit and implied. Vallandingham could not forget a wrong. He would not forgive an injury. He voted for Pendleton and favored Chase, and helped kill the former with the latter. After a prolonged contest, Pendleton was beaten, and Seymour and Blair were nominated on a platform that induced their defeat.

The "Negro" and the "Confederate Brigadier" became the scare-crows that the two great parties used to keep their wavering followers in line. The Republican ticket, headed by I. R. Sherwood, carried Ohio in October by 17,500 majority, and a month later Gen. Grant polled 280,167 votes and the Democrats cast 238,621 for Seymour. The Republican vote increased 13,000 in four weeks and the Democratic vote fell off 11,000, a fact that shows the heavy load the Democrats were carrying in the campaign, both as to platform and candidates. The total vote, 518,788, was the largest ever cast up to that time. In 1869, the Republicans nominated R. B. Hayes for Governor and the Democrats placed Geo. H. Pendleton at the head of their ticket. Hayes polled 235,081 and beat Pendleton by 7,501 votes after an exciting campaign. In 1870 the Republicans carried the state by a plurality of 16,695. In 1871, Edward F. Noyes, as the Republican candidate for Governor, defeated Geo. W. McCook, who headed the Democratic ticket, by 20,168 votes, Gideon T. Stewart, the Prohibition candidate, polling 4,084 votes.

Under the able and splendid leadership of Vallandingham, the Ohio Democracy made its "New Departure" in 1871 and declared in favor of accepting the war legislation, as embodied in the three last amendments to the constitution, as a finality. The Democrats in other states followed the lead of Ohio Democrats. This movement was the forerunner of the Liberal movement in 1872, which prepared the way for the return of many able and influential men to the fold of Democracy, from which they had been driven by slavery and the war.

It would be interesting to give a detailed history of the changing phases and fortunes of parties and politics at this time, but it is not the purpose of the author, nor is it within the scope of this work. We are hastily following the trail of events, that we may properly trace the causes that led to the advent of "Boodle."

VIII. The jealousy of the states to preserve their rights and identity, and to prevent the influence of national on state affairs, made them hold their elections for state officers apart from the Federal elections. In 1872, North Carolina voted in August, Vermont and Maine in September, and Pennsylvania, Ohio and Indiana in October. The results in these states foreshadowed the defeat of Greeley. The states gradually changed their constitutions and held their state elections in November, upon the same day that the Federal elections were held. Ohio was the last to abandon her October elections, and the concentration of all the efforts, money and men of the various political organizations, upon this advanced outpost, led the people to adopt an amendment to the Constitution, making the change in 1887. In October, 1872, the Republicans polled 265,830 votes, the Democrats 251,780, Independent 2,045. In November, Grant polled 281,852, Greeley 244,321, and scattering 3,325. The overwhelming victory of Gen. Grant, after a most violent and bitterly contested campaign, assured the Republicans of the continued confidence of the people, and the undisputed control of all departments of the government. But in less than a year the country was convulsed by a panic, that was the legitimate result of trifling with the laws that govern an honest and wise financial system. A contraction of the large volume of paper currency had been begun as a step toward the resumption of specie payment. By stealth and without that debate in Congress, or discussion in the press, that the importance of the subject demanded, silver had been stricken down by demonetization and one-half or more of the redemption money of the country, had been dishonored and reduced to servitude as token money, and by methods unworthy of a great people and an honest monetary system, the way had been surreptitiously prepared for the resumption of specie payments in *gold.* So quietly and cunningly had this great crime been committed, that many members of Congress and even the President of the United States in signing the bill, were not cognizant of the fact.

Greenbackism became rampant, and under public clamor and the general distress, Congress and the President both yielded, and the volume of paper money which had been restricted, was increased. The Democrats of Ohio adopted a platform in favor of the "rag baby." That was a wide departure from all the moorings of a past once glorious in the history of a party that had never deserted the sound teachings of experience and the Constitution. The convention called from a long retirement as their standard bearer, one of "the people from the southward," Wm. Allen, of Ross, one of the most romantic and classical figures in Ohio politics. He had made his last appearance in public life, as a member of the United States Senate, during James K. Polk's brilliant administration. Mr. Allen had lived so long in the peace and quiet of his rural home, on the beautiful hills in the Scioto valley, that he was unknown to the present generation. His reappearance upon the national stage was like a ghost of another age. But he proved a very lively ghost. After his first speech at Columbus, Oliver P. Morton committed the unfortunate blunder of sneering at the "palsied old man," and the result was a vigorous reply as to Gov. Morton's physical condition, that aroused the state and called forth many a mossback to the polls, who had quietly been awaiting the final summons of all. Gov. Allen's opponent was Gov. E. F. Noyes, a man of ordinary mind and few intellectual qualities, but gifted with a magnificent pair of lungs, and a great voice. In a total vote of 448,878, Allen received 214,654; Noyes 213,837; Stewart, Prohibition, 10,278; Collins, labor candidate, 10,109. Gov. Allen was the only one on the Democratic state ticket elected, thanks to Gov. Morton's untimely sneer, and Gov. Noyes' weak record. The Democrats carried the Legislature, and Allen G. Thurman was re-elected to the United States Senate. In 1874, the Democrats carried Ohio again, polling 238,405 votes, to 221,204 cast for the Republican ticket, and 7,815 votes for the Prohibition candidate.

In 1875, R. B. Hayes, who had left Cincinnati, and was living in Fremont, was called for a third term to head the Republican ticket against Gov. Allen. The currency question was the leading issue. The battle was a royal contest, and the largest vote ever cast in Ohio was polled, 592,700. Of this number, Hayes polled 297,817; Allen 292,273, and 2,610 scattering. The importance of this fight led to the liberal contributions inside and more especially outside of the state, from bankers, office holders and others interested, and for the first time in the history of Ohio politics, money from abroad was used to insure success. It is not charged that any money was used corruptly in this campaign, or in such quantities as to change the result, but for the first time it became an important factor in the result, under the direction and advice of such brilliant and practical manipulators as Charles Foster. Gov. Hayes' triumph made him the Republican candidate for the Presidency, against Gov. Samuel J. Tilden, in 1876. Money was the chief campaign argument on both sides in Ohio, in the eventful campaign of 1876. It was used to bring out and poll every vote that money by any means, could get. The result was two perfect party organizations, and the vote was an honest expression of the will of the people, but it was the beginning, in a large measure, of "Bosses and Boodle," and the dawn of a system in which political organization and manipulation became a paying business.

At the October election, the Republicans polled 317,856 votes, and the Democrats received 311,220, scattering 1863, and in November this was increased to 330,698 votes for R. B. Hayes, 323,182 votes for S. J. Tilden, and 5,891 scattering; a total of 659,771 votes. Hayes' plurality was 7,516, the smallest ever given a Republican-candidate for the Presidency in the largest total vote ever cast in the state. The long dispute over the result of the Presidential election, demoralized the people and parties. In 1877, in a contest for governor, R. M. Bishop, the Democratic candidate, received 271,625 votes, and defeated Wm. H. West, the Republican candidate, who received 249,105 votes, while 34,237 were divided between three other candidates. The Democrats carried the legislature and Geo. H. Pendleton was elected to the United States Senate.

The refusal of Allen G. Thurman to endorse the Greenback doctrine as urged by Washington McLean, and advocated by the Cincinnati *Enquirer*, had led to a breach, and for years Thurman was bitterly opposed and constantly pursued by the McLeans, father and son, Washington, John, and their newspaper. Mr. John R. McLean, about 1872, had succeeded his father and associates in the ownership and management of the Cincinnati *Enquirer*, and for years this influential but erratic and uncertain newspaper, was destined to exert a wide, dangerous and demoralizing influence upon the politics and Democrats of Ohio.

In 1878, with the silver question for the first time making its appearance as an issue before the people, the Republicans carried Ohio, by less than 4,000 plurality. The head of the ticket polled 274,120 votes, to 271,625 cast for David R. Paige, while 44,014 votes were cast for two other candidates. The advent of David R. Paige in Ohio politics, marks the advent of an important character. He is the forerunner of Democratic Boodle. He became later its chief dispenser. There was but little money used in the campaign in which he was defeated for Secretary of State, by such a small margin. He was a prosperous and respected young business man in Akron, O., when he entered upon the fatal paths of politics. He became a large contractor on public works in West Virginia. He was elected to Congress in 1882 from the Akron district, and served one term. In 1883-4 he was the Boss and Master Boodler in the Payne Purchase. He removed to New York City, where he became interested in large contracts. He became involved. He raised large sums of money by forgery, and failed He fled the country, leaving family and relations amidst the ruin wrought by his dishonesty, and to face the shame and bear the punishment for his misdeeds. His brother was involved and sent to the state prison for defrauding those who had trusted him, and has but recently been paroled, and permitted to rejoin his heart-broken family. David R. Paige is a criminal and a fugitive in a strange land, overtaken by a just retribution for the crimes he committed as a Boss and a Boodler.

BOODLE NYMPHS SEDUCING CALVIN $ BRICE.

(*Porcupine, Dec. 1889.*)

CHAPTER VI.

OVER THE FALLS INTO THE WHIRLPOOL OF CORRUPTION.—CHARLES FOSTER'S POLITICS, CAMPAIGNS AND METHODS.

WE need not stop to enquire whether any immediate danger menaces the institutions of the country. It is enough to ask ourselves whether it can be justly said, that the great public trust of suffrage is being wisely administered, and whether its exercise is securing good government to the masses of the people. And in so far as it is not, it is the duty of all good citizens to arraign suffrage at the bar of public opinion, to give an account of its stewardship.

How is suffrage organized and registered? Is it done as in the simple days of the Republic? Is it done deliberately and honestly at all? Not that thousands do not vote considerately and conscientiously. Of course they do. But the question is, are the methods and appliances for carrying elections conducive to, or even intended to produce, a full and fair expression of the popular will, and by that expression to secure the best government for the people?

If that be the object, the means used would seem to be singularly inappropriate, and the result singularly deficient. A full and fair vote is what the whole people, as well as the "political people," have a right to demand; and legislation for the masses, not for the classes, is the mandate of free government.

"It is undoubtly true, however, that to all free governments, parties are an inseparable incident, and serve in many instances a salutary purpose. And it is equally true that all parties must have some system of organization and concentration of action. And it must also be conceded, that as voters consist of every class of society, all can not be influenced by like arguments, or brought into action by like inducements. An appeal to principle may be sufficient for one, while another can only be moved by playing on his prejudices. And so, too, candidates often influence voters by mere personal popularity, without reference to the principles they profess, or even to their essential fitness for the place. There must, therefore, be more or less laxity in the methods of political action. All these things show the difficulties of self-government, and should arouse the intelligent voter to meet and overcome them. You are members of the electoral college, and are bound by every consideration that can address itself to freemen to perform your own duty, and require every other man to perform his. The officers you choose, make or administer the laws. How are officers made? The primaries are held to choose delegates to a convention. The primaries are manipulated by the "Bosses," large and small, of party "rings." Thousands of the best citizens all over the country never go near them. The "workers," by personal importunity or influence over the bread of the humble laborer, or through the dram shop, or by ready cash, can too often control votes enough at the primary to put in their men, and fix the convention for their candidate. The "Boss of the machine" becomes the master of the party, and throws his toils around all public officers and dictates all public policies.

"GREASE FOR THE WHEELS."

"Then comes the canvass and the election. Whatever else may be involved, the "spoils of office" are at stake. The henchmen of the chiefs are looking for their share of the booty, and why should they not be? Have not most of those who have wielded power for years past, gone in poor and come out rich? And is it not the laborer who helps to make the millionaire worthy of his hire? Do they not know, does the country not know, that few who have ruled long at the Federal Capital, have failed to become rich? Money, therefore, becomes the motive power of the election. And can you expect that in a community, whose ruling thought is haste to get rich, condemnation will come to the candidate who stakes his all—and all his friends can raise—to secure a prize where there may be "millions in it"? My friends, the use of money at elections must be stopped, or our Republic cannot endure. *He who bribes to be elected, is ready to be bribed after he is.*

"But the evil does not stop here. Profit, not honor, becomes the motive to candidacy. The candidate must be rich enough to bear his assessment and the capable poor must be excluded. High statesmanship is ended; personal aggrandizement is inaugurated. The officer must make back what he spent for his election, and public taxes are his spoils. He lives by the "machine." As of old, he shouts: "Great is Diana of the Ephesians." Patronage becomes power. An army of one hundred thousand office holders are taxed as their tenure of office, and they pay their assessments out of the taxes the people pay into the treasury. Their assessments are expended in the interest of the "machine." The voter is the vassal of the office holder. The office holder is the vassal of the "Boss." The President is the lord paramount of his mesne lord, the "Boss." When a chief magistrate refuses to a "Boss" Senator the dispensation of patronage in aid of his own aspirations, and in reward for the power of his "ring" in carrying a State and making that chief magistrate, like the turbulent barons of old, he rebels, and indignantly resigns his place in the Senate. Under this new feudal system the workers swear fealty to the "Bosses," and the "Bosses" own the rulers. Still this evil, great as it is, might be borne. Who holds the offices if they be well administered is of small moment. Nevertheless, as men must be the agencies through which all administration is carried on, their ability and purity are matters of the first importance."—*Speech of Gen. Durbin Ward, delivered at Hamilton, O., July 4, 1882.*

In his "Twenty Years in Congress," Mr. James G. Blaine, very conveniently for himself, and very happily for his party, closes the period with the advent of President Garfield's administration, from 1861 to 1881. He says: "The twenty years form indeed an incomparable era in the history of the United States." "It is difficult to estimate the progress of the people of the United States, in intelligence and in wealth, since the close of the Civil War." "The progress of the American people in wealth is beyond precedent." "Nor have these twenty years been distinguished only by the acquisition of wealth; no period of our history has been more marked by *generous* expenditures for worthy ends." The doleful plaint of the "Tribune of the people," Durbin Ward, which heads this chapter, is a companion-piece to Mr. Blaine's picture of our unexampled wealth and prosperity. The rapid accumulations of wealth in the hands of the favored few is the natural result of laws offering great inducements to money and stimulating industries. Temptations crowd around such opportunities too strong for humanity to resist, and too powerful to be abashed by the penalties of feeble laws, which are only a protest and never a prevention of such a class of crimes. These crimes were unknown before the war. A train of evils with brazen front and pompous tread follows in the wake of our boasted prosperity. Men arise who are no longer restrained by virtue and conscience, but who are willing to use this hastily acquired wealth to debauch the people, and corrupt the right of franchise, to advance their own personal interests and ambitions. There is no more signal illustration of this fact than the political career of Charles Foster, of Fostoria, O. His parents came from Massachusetts early in this century. He was born in Seneca County, April 12, 1828, in the place founded and named by his father. He was given an ordinary education. His was one of those genial natures that would never have survived a collegiate course. His father taught him to share his business cares from early youth. In a country store of a growing and prosperous agricultural country, he learned to study human nature and to weigh the hidden motives that move men even in the common affairs of life. His ideas broadened as he grew to manhood, and such was his capacity for affairs, and devotion to the details of business, that his father's business became his own. When the war began, Charles Foster was in the prime of young manhood, and in the midst of a successful business career. He had no taste for battle-fields or glory. His keen and calculating mind early discovered the opportunities presented by a changing market and rising prices, occasioned by the war and augmented by the tariff legislation of Congress, and he was swift to act, and greatly profited by his investments. As he prospered, he and father branched out into many lines of business and investments. They started a bank, which for years was the custodian of the money and possessed the confidence of the people from all the surrounding country. He encouraged manufacturing enterprises. He became interested in railroads, and induced no less than three lines to build through Fostoria.

Up to the evil hour that first tempted him into the field of politics, no man in the new northwestern counties of Ohio had contributed more to their material advancement and rapid development than Charles Foster. He was deservedly popular. He had a noble and generous heart. He never said "No" to a worthy applicant of any kind. His standing in the financial world grew as his affairs prospered. His word was better than a bond. He was affable in manner, easy of approach, and always cheerful. His presence was the sunshine that dispels the gloom that hangs over and darkens so many lives. His first appearance in politics was after the war, when he made a hopeless race on the Republican ticket for State Senator, in the strong Democratic counties of Seneca, Crawford and Wyandot. He was beaten but not dishonored. The vote he polled indicated his great popularity, and later led to his nomination for Congress, in 1870. The Democratic candidate was Edward F. Dickinson, of Sandusky, who had served one term in Congress, and had endeared himself to his party by his steady and uniform opposition to all the "war measures," but unfortunately he was addicted to excess in drink. Mr. Foster carried his business methods into politics. He was thorough, and neglected none of the details of organization that have revolutionized political methods in Ohio. He was most liberal in his allowances to local committees, but he did not depend upon these common instruments of parties to secure results. He had his personal agents, who did "missionary" work of a very effective kind in every township in the district. Foster polled 13,274 votes to 12,498 polled for his opponent, and defeated Judge Dickinson by 776 votes. The Democrats of the district were dumbfounded by the result. It was entirely unexpected. The drift was all in their favor. In a light vote the Republicans had carried the state by less than 15,000 plurality. In Crawford County Foster ran 10 votes behind the state ticket. In Erie County he ran 187 votes ahead; in Huron County he ran 52 ahead; in Ottawa he ran 35 ahead; in Sandusky he ran 59 behind his ticket, and in Seneca he ran 161 votes ahead. His splendid canvass had helped the state ticket, and transformed a Democratic stronghold into a Republican district. The counties comprising the district, and the votes cast in the contest of 1870, were as follows:

	FOSTER.	DICKINSON.
Crawford	1,613	2,461
Erie	2,735	1,260
Huron	3,344	1,939
Ottawa	791	1,148
Sandusky	1,940	2,670
Seneca	2,851	3,020
Totals	13,274	12,498

Charles Foster made his appearance on the stormy national arena, in the 42d Congress. James G. Blaine was chosen Speaker over Geo. W. Morgan of Ohio, receiving 126 votes, to 92 cast for Morgan. Among Mr. Foster's colleagues from Ohio, were Gen. John Beatty of Marion, John A. Bingham of Harrison, Chas. N. Lamison of Allen, James Monroe of Lorain, L. D. Campbell of Butler, James A. Garfield of Portage, Geo. W. Morgan of Knox, Ozra J. Dodds and Aaron F. Perry from the two Cincinnati districts,

Frank McKinney of Miami, Samuel Shellabarger of Clarke, and P. Van Trump of Fairfield. Upon Mr. Foster's appearance in Congress, Mr. Blaine says: "Charles Foster came from the north-western section of Ohio, in which his father had been one of the pioneers and founders of the town Fostoria. He attracted more than the ordinary attention given to new members, from the fact that he had been able to carry a Democratic district, and, for a young man, to exert a large influence on public opinion. He was distinguished by strong common sense, by a popular manner, by *personal generosity*, and by a quick instinct as to the expediency of political measures and the strength of political parties. These qualities at once gave him a position of consequence in the House, superior to that held by many of the older members of established reputation. His subsequent career vindicated his early promise, and enabled him to lead the Republican party of Ohio to victory, in more than one canvass, which at the outset was surrounded with doubt and danger." During his first term, he served upon the Committee upon Claims. The war amendments to the Constitution were clinched by the Civil Rights bill, which was passed during Mr. Foster's first term, and in deference to public opinion, an amnesty bill was passed restoring to citizenship all but about 700 persons who had been outlawed by the third section of the Fourteenth amendment. Being of a liberal disposition and a frank and open nature, and representing a Democratic district, Mr. Foster was more advanced than his party, and he made many friends among the Southern members of Congress by his open advocacy of a generous policy toward the South and its leaders.

The "Salary grab," was passed by this Congress. An act that aroused the public indignation of the North, and did much to shake the confidence of the people in the Republican majority. Mr. Foster was too shrewd a politician, and understood the temper of the people too well, to be caught taking money he did not earn. Such members from Ohio as Lamison, and McKinney needed the "back pay," and took it, and by doing so, signed their political deathwarrants.

II. In 1872, the Ohio Legislature, being Republican, passed an act re-districting the state. The Democratic counties of Ottawa and Crawford were taken off of the Foster district, and the county of Hancock, in which Mr. Foster had many personal friends and interests, was added. This left the district with a small Democratic majority; with the two rockribbed counties of Ottawa and Crawford detached, the task of carrying the district was made lighter, and it was one that Mr. Foster felt equal to. He was nominated by the Republicans, and the Democrats and Liberals put up as his opponent, Rush R. Sloan, of Erie. However solemn and mournful the campaign may have been in the other sections of the state, on account of Horace Greeley's nomination, the contest in the Tenth district was not a lifeless one. The Democrats had selected as a standard bearer, a man who would "fight the devil with fire," and money flowed like water. There never was such a contest before in Ohio, and there have been few like it since. Foster was met with his own methods, but he did not shrink from the issue.* The two parties spent not less than $60,000 in the campaign, and this came chiefly from the two candidates. It was an open sale—a public auction, and the goods were knocked down to the highest bidder. Foster was elected over Sloan by 726 votes. The vote by counties was as follows:

	FOSTER.	SLOAN.
Erie	2,877	2,701
Hancock	2,384	2,641
Huron	3,939	2,433
Sandusky	2,468	2,910
Seneca	3,329	3,536
Totals	14,997	14,271

Mr. Blaine was elected speaker of the House in the 43rd Congress, and Mr. Foster placed upon the Ways and Means Committee. A most important place for a comparatively new member. Among the new members who made their appearance in the House from Ohio, was Hugh J. Jewett, from the capital district, who did not serve out his term, but resigned to accept the presidency of the Erie railroad, and joined

* Mr. Sloan, in 1880, told the writer that he spent $20,000 in his campaign, and said Mr. Foster spent $35,000, and was elected by buying two townships in Huron County.

the Ohio Colony in New York City. Lorenzo Danford came from the Belmont district, Gen. Jas. W. Robinson from the Hardin district, M. L. Southard from Zanesville, R. S. Parsons from Cleveland, and Milton Sayler and Gen. Henry B. Banning from Cincinnati.

This Congress, the 43rd, passed the act demonetizing silver, a fact that did not become generally known until several years afterwards. The panic broke upon the country, and swept the Democrats into power in many states. Mr. Foster made little noise, and attended to routine duties during this Congress. In 1874 he was a candidate again. The Democrats were eager for the fray, and sanguine of certain success. The tide was all in their favor. They selected as a candidate, Geo. E. Seney, a lawyer of good repute having a paying practice, popular and not a pauper. He did not attempt to beat his opponent at his own methods. On his part the campaign was not a money one. If it had been, he would have been beaten, for when a candidate is compelled to buy his own partisans to vote their own ticket, it is difficult to tell how many to buy, or how much to pay. Mr. Foster defeated Mr. Seney by 159 votes. The vote by counties was as follows:

	FOSTER.	SENEY.
Erie	2,619	2,105
Hancock	2,297	2,415
Huron	3,423	2,409
Sandusky	2,239	2,969
Seneca	3,200	3,721
Totals	13,778	13,619

This was the closest race Mr. Foster had yet had. He polled 1,200 votes less than he received two years before, and there were 289 votes cast for a third candidate, but he had succeeded by a meager plurality of 159, and he alone can tell approximately the amount of money he had expended to secure his third election. For the first time since the first election of Abraham Lincoln, the Republicans had lost the control of the House of Representatives. The resumption act was agreed upon in caucus, and became a law in January, 1875, before the new Democratic House, elected the previous fall, came upon the scene. The forty-fourth Congress met March 6, 1875, and M. S. Kerr, of Indiana, was elected speaker of the House, receiving 173 votes to 106 cast for James G. Blaine. Mr. Foster retired from the Committee on Ways and Means, and was placed upon the Appropriation Committee, on which he served during this and the succeeding House, when he retired from Congress.

Among the new members from Ohio, who appeared in this Congress, was Henry B. Payne, who succeeded R. S. Parsons from Cleveland, and John R. McMahon from the old Vallandingham district. On the advent of this Congress, the capitol and the country were in a feverish and unsettled state. All kinds of corruption were charged against officials in every branch of the government, and these charges were often well founded and generally believed. The time of the House was taken up in investigations, and personal debates of the most exciting character, in which Mr. Blaine figured as the leader and the star on the Republican side. Boss Shephard and the Washington ring were in the midst of their harvest. To have held office during the past few years, was a seemingly just ground of being a suspect of corruption, if not proven. The storm centered around the unfortunate and indiscreet Secretary of War, Belknap, who resigned his office and was impeached. This performance appeased and soothed the public mind.

III. Among the unique characters in this House was James Williams, of the Vincennes district, Indiana. He was a farmer. He dressed in plain, old-fashioned "blue jeans." He wore a collar and stock, was tall and angular, awkward and uncouth, but he had strong common sense and a fund of humor and anecdote that gave him an honorable recognition among his associates. He bore a striking resemblance to Lincoln. He was chairman of the Commitee on Claims, and he attempted to curtail the expenses of the House. The amount of expenditures for "lemons, ice, sugar, and things," had run up into the thousands. His efforts at economy were met with ridicule by the Republicans as a "pea-nut" policy. Among the leaders in this assault was Charles Foster. It was foreign to his nature to sneer at any one, and his early life and training had taught him the virtues of saving and economy. But four years of life at the capitol had wrought a revolution in Mr. Foster's personal views and habits. Late suppers and receptions, champagne and draw-poker, dress-suits and society had led Mr. Foster to forget those honest days in his own career, when he wore a "gallus" over his shoulder at the mill, and picked his teeth with a splinter from a rail. He attempted to belittle "Blue Jeans" Williams' attempt at economy, and his sneer provoked a reply from the plain old farmer that was cruel and crushing. Charles Foster's sneer at Mr. Williams led to his nomination and election as Governor of Indiana, in the Presidential campaign of 1876.

IV. It was evident to Republicans that their party supremacy was at an end, if Ohio were lost. Wm. Allen was Governor, and was to be the candidate of the Democrats in 1875, and it would require a good man and extraordinary effort to defeat him. Charles Foster had become a power in Ohio politics, and he undertook the management of a preliminary campaign, that led to the nomination and election of R. B. Hayes as Governor in 1875, and this success made the latter Republican candidate for President in 1876, and placed him in the White House in 1877.

Judge Alphonso Taft, of Cincinnati, was a candidate for the Republican nomination for Governor. Both Governors Noyes and Hayes had declined to be candidates, and it looked as if there would be no opposition to Judge Taft, but the "Pope's Big Toe" made its appearance in Ohio politics, and Judge Taft's opposition to the enforced use of the Bible in the public schools made him a victim to the popular frenzy. Foster skillfully worked up this feeling to the detriment of Judge Taft. Pretending to favor his canvass, he wrote him a letter as to his position upon the Catholics and the public schools, and he received a frank and manly reply. This Mr. Foster produced and had read in the convention, and the result was what he desired and expected, for the apprehension of the delegates was aroused, and the name of Mr. Hayes was sprung upon the convention, and Judge Taft, instead of being nominated without opposition, was badly beaten, securing less than 150 votes out of a total of 600, and Mr. Hayes was nominated by acclamation. In 1876 Mr. Foster was nominated a fourth time for Congress. His opponent was a John H. Hudson, a grain merchant and respectable business man of Sandusky City. The campaign resembled those that preceded it, but in some respects it proved the hardest contest Mr. Foster had ever had. The Democrats expected to elect a President and were hopeful and united. Their organization was superb and was backed by ample funds provided by Mr. Hudson. Mr. Foster's congressional record was attacked with telling effect, but he knew every inch of the ground and every person in the district, and by a careful canvass he knew the strength of his opponent and his own weakness. The Democrats carried the district in October and November, and Mr. Foster ran ahead of his ticket and beat Mr. Hudson by 271 votes. In one locality, young men who were casting their first votes, were paid five dollars each to vote for Mr. Foster for Congress. The following is the result by counties:

	FOSTER.	HUDSON.
Erie	3,178	3,157
Hancock	2,801	3,114
Huron	4,432	2,936
Sandusky	2,948	3,498
Seneca	3,965	4,348
Totals	17,324	17,053

This ends the sucsessful boodle campaigns in the old Tenth District. The Democrats carried the Legislature in 1877, and in 1878 the state was redistricted and Mr. Foster was placed in a district composed of the counties of Crawford, Hardin, Marion, Morrow, Seneca and Wyandot. In 1878 he made his last Congressional race in this district, and was beaten. He ran ahead of his ticket, but either his "bar'l" was too small, or the Democratic majority was too large or too high priced to buy. There were 1,148 votes scattering; the Democrats polled 16,273 votes and Mr. Foster polled 14,982, and he made his exit from the stage of national politics after eight years of service in a very critical and memorable period of our Congressional history.

V. Let us now approach one of the most alarming

events in our national history, known as "the fraud of 1876." We shall only deal with the details of this period of our political history so far as they relate to Mr. Foster. In dealing with him as a public character, who has attained his eminence and his honors by great wealth, and its corruptions in politics, it is a matter of simple justice, not only to portray the good qualities of such a character, but to dwell on those acts in his official and public career, that may in some measure compensate for the wrongs he has done his country and his age, and the crimes he has committed against public policy and political morals.

During President Johnson's term of office, Gen. Grant was modest, wise and discreet. As soon as he had reached this great office himself, his character seemed to undergo a sudden change. His mind, like that of all great military characters, was not used to the genius and purpose of laws. In war he was governed by conditions, and not laws. His genius was his only law, and success had given him faith in his infallibility. The Tenure-of-office act had been passed by the Republicans to prevent Mr. Johnson from removing their partisans from office. It was a fight for the spoils. It was not an edifying spectacle. For an alleged violation of this act, articles of impeachment were presented against Mr. Johnson, and an attempt was made to depose him from his high office. Fortunately the attempt failed by a narrow margin.

Five days after Gen. Grant succeeded President Johnson, under the suspension of the rules, on motion of Benj. Butler, the House of Representatives passed a bill to repeal this act. The Senate was not equally expeditious, but within a few weeks the teeth of the act were pulled, and the removal of the obnoxious Johnsonites from office began.

President Grant's scheme for the annexation of San Domingo, which was rejected by the Senate in June, 1870, was the beginning of a breach in the Republican party, which grew to alarming proportions. It first resulted in the Liberal disaffection, and then in the factions known as the "Stalwarts," and "Half Breeds," or Grant and Anti-Grant. Charles Sumner, as chairman on the Committee on Foreign Relations, made a speech arraigning the administration in his pompous and ponderous style. It hurt. President Grant had been the popular ideal since the war. He was fresh from a camp where his word was obeyed, and all were subordinates, and where to question was mutiny. He looked upon Senator Sumner's acts as such, and proceeded, through his political friends, to punish Mr. Sumner accordingly. When the first Congress to which Charles Foster was elected met and organized, March 4, 1871, the country was astounded by the removal of Charles Sumner from the head of the Committee on Foreign Relations. This was done by a caucus of Republican Senators, to please President Grant. This was a brutal act, and a causeless and needless humiliation to one of the great characters of Congress. It was a blow from which Mr. Sumner never recovered. This was the first gun fired and the attacks began in earnest upon the administration. Open charges of corruption were publicly made against some of President Grant's favorites and personal friends. These charges the Liberals crystalized in the Cincinnati platform in 1872 as a justification of their conduct. President Grant's triumphant election for a second term, brought a lull in the assaults upon himself and his administration. But when it broke forth it was with greater violence and more damaging than ever. The success of the Democrats in 1874, enabled many Republicans who were opposed to the administration, but did not wish to appear as its assailants within their own party, to mask their purposes, and encourage and instigate charges and investigations. Mr. Foster's sympathies and associates were with Mr. Blaine and his friends, who were opposed to President Grant. Mr. Foster had sided with the Democrats in one of the complications in the state affairs of Louisana, and became very friendly and intimate with some of the Southern members of Congress. As President Grant's administration grew older, there were fears freely expressed and publicly proclaimed, that he would be a candidate for a third term. Upon his return to the Senate in 1875, Ex-President Johnson, in a speech openly charged President Grant with being a candidate for third term, and thought our liberties were menaced by his administration.

Gen. Frank Blair, a Senator from Missouri, had written a letter exposing President Grant's character and ambitions, and predicted that he would never leave the White House "until he was carried out feet foremost." Many people believed this. But if President Grant ever had, at this time, any designs upon a third term, the exposures made by a Democratic House of Representatives, with the aid of their Republican allies, who wanted to kill Grant off, laid his ambition to rest. Public prejudice and opposition made it evident that he could not accomplish his designs by the regular avenues of party machinery, such as had twice secured his nomination and election. President Grant was not a candidate in 1876. He was in 1880, and failed. Garfield's assassination and death was the legitimate result of an interminable struggle that had been going on inside the Republican party for over ten years. In the contest for the Republican nomination for the Presidency in 1876, Mr. Foster preferred Mr. Blaine, but was not averse to nor downcast over the selection of Mr. Hayes. He had forced Mr. Hayes from retirement the year before, when Bill Allen and the rag-baby were laid away to rest in a common political grave. The Democrats nominated Samuel J. Tilden, and adopted an excellent platform. The contest was a masterly one. The result in the October states did not foreshadow the result as formerly. In Indiana, "Blue Jeans" Williams defeated Benjamin Harrison for Governor, by 5000 plurality, and the Republicans carried Mr. Hayes' state, Ohio, by about 9000 votes. All parties paused to look over the October battle-fields, and when the results were known, they renewed the conflict with tremendous vigor throughout the country. When the polls were closed, the returns clearly indicated the election of Mr. Tilden. He had carried the solid South, New York, New Jersey, Connecticut, and Indiana, but the next day Mr. Chandler, the Chairman of the Republican National Committee, telegraphed from New York City that Mr. Hayes had received 185 electoral votes and was elected. This claim astonished the Democrats and aroused the whole country. The Republicans claimed the electoral votes of South Carolina, Florida and Louisiana, and the election of Mr. Hayes by one vote. Of course the Democrats disputed this. Great excitement ensued. The leaders and partisans of both parties were wild and indiscreet. The Democrats held meetings. They charged fraud. The Republicans denied it. Resolutions were adopted, pledging thousands of armed men to go to the Capital and seat the Democratic claimant. Riot, revolution and bloodshed seemed to be a foregone conclusion. President Grant smoked and said little. His opportunity was at hand. Prominent men of both parties were sent South to watch the count. Mr.

Hayes was silent. If he was not honestly elected, he did not want the office and would not claim it. Mr. Tilden was active but secretive in his endeavors both to arouse public indignation and make good his title to the office. He wanted the great prize dearly, but he was not willing to fight for it. His friends tried to purchase it for him. They failed. Treason meant death, and in such a crisis there are no sums that can tempt partisans, however cheap and dishonest they may be on ordinary occasions.

On November 10th, a few days after the election, President Grant sent his famous order to Gen. Sherman, saying: "Instruct Gen. Augur, in Lousiana, and Gen. Ruger, in Florida, to be vigilant with the force at their command to preserve peace and good order, and to see that the proper and legal boards of canvassers are unmolested in the performance of their duties. Should there be any grounds of suspicion of a fraudulent count, on either side, *it should be reported and denounced at once.* No man worthy of the office of President should be willing to hold it if counted in or placed there by fraud. Either party can afford to be disappointed in the result. The country can not afford to have the result tainted by the suspicion of illegal or false returns." This was a most extraordinary document to emanate from the chief executive of a free people under any circumstances. The President made the military authorities a judicial tribunal to hear and decide a cause at law. The several returning boards certified the returns in favor of the Hayes electors. The electors met December 6th in the various states, and Hayes received 185 votes and Tilden 184. The dispute continued, although public excitement in a measure subsided. Congress met the first week in December. President Grant concentrated the troops around Washington to "suppress disorder." His message and his attitude alarmed thoughtful men of all parties, and hastened the agreement that resulted in the electoral count by a commission composed of five members of the House, five Senators, and five Judges of the Supreme Court. The demand for a compromise came first from the South. Randall L. Gibson, of Lousiana, presented a memorial to the House demanding the passage of a bill to provide a plan for counting the electoral vote. Charles Foster had pointed out to his Southern friends the danger of President Grant's position, and the certainty of riot and chaos. They could gain nothing by resisting a compromise. If Grant held on until there was a peaceful adjustment they would be deprived of the control of their own states. If they agreed to compromise, by a lawful method, whoever was declared elected would succeed Grant. They were assured that if Hayes was seated they should be permitted to retain control of their state governments. They had faith in Mr. Foster's word. He was backed by Stanley Matthews. The bill became a law. In the

House 160 Democrats and 31 Republicans voted for the bill, and 17 Democrats and 69 Republicans against the bill. In the Senate 26 Democrats and 21 Republicans voted for the bill, and 1 Democrat and 16 Republicans voted against it. Three Ohio men served on the commission, Senator Allen G. Thurman, H. B. Payne and James A. Garfield. By a vote of 8 to 7, Mr. Hayes was declared elected. He was inaugurated. He took the oath Sunday, March 4, but was publicly inaugurated Monday, March 5, 1877. Charles Foster, by his good judgment, shrewd management, and good faith, had aided to save our institutions from the most terrible strain they had ever been subjected to. The Democrats took possession of the state governments in all of the disputed states. In Lousiana Gov. Packard claimed to have received 12,000 more votes than Mr. Hayes, but the Democratic candidate, Gov. F. T. Nicolls, was installed as Governor. Of this transaction James G. Blaine says:

"No act of President Hayes did so much to create a discontent within the ranks of the Republican party. No act of his did so much to give color to the thousand rumors that filled the political atmosphere, touching a bargain between the President's friends and some Southern leaders, pending the decision of the Electoral Commission. The election of the President and the election of Mr. Packard, rested substantially upon the same foundation, and many Republicans felt that the President's refusal to recognize Mr.

Packard as Governor of Louisiana, furnished ground to his enemies for disputing his own election. Having been placed in the Presidency by a title as strong as could be confirmed under the Constitution and laws of the country, it was, in the judgment of the majority of the Republican party, an unwise and unwarranted act on the part of the President to purchase peace in the South, by surrendering Louisiana to the Democratic party."

Had Mr. Blaine told what he knew about this transaction, it would have made a very valuable and interesting portion of his history of our politics. It is most unfortunate that the few Statesmen who become historians, feel a delicacy in giving the facts about such important transactions.

VI. Mr. Foster was not long idle. He was defeated for Congress in 1878, and his term expired March 4, 1879, and he immediately began a quiet and effective campaign for the nomination for governor, using the methods within his own party, that he had used so frequently against the Democrats. Among the members of the Ohio Legislature, elected in 1877, was John Seitz, a farmer from Seneca county, who had been elected to the Senate as a Democrat, from Mr. Foster's Senatorial district. Mr. Seitz was a farmer. He had served as a member of the Ohio House of Representatives, and since his last appearance in the Senate, in '78-'79, he has joined the Labor and the Populist party. In 1881 he was a candidate for Governor against Foster and Bookwalter, and polled 6,330 votes. In 1887 he was again a candidate against Foraker and Powell, and polled 24,711 votes. He is a man of more than average intelligence, with strong convictions and restricted views upon public questions. He was a useful member of the Legislature. He had known the Fosters, father and son, for years. He had had ample opportunity to study the methods of the younger Foster in politics. Brilliant and effective as they were, generous and convincing as they ever proved, Mr. Seitz in his simplicity had permitted himself to become prejudiced against the Fostorian school of politics. Mr. Seitz was firmly of the opinion that if the evils that fall around in the wake of Mr. Foster's political activity, were not restrained or prevented, that the ballot would become a farce. In 1878 he introduced in the Senate, S. B. No. 85, "To Preserve the Purity of Elections." The bill was referred to the Committee on Elections, and there died.

In 1878, in Mr. Foster's last race for Congress, great as was the majority against him, and aided by the unpopular candidate, E. B. Finley, he succeeded in thoroughly frightening his opponent and his party, but his lavish use of money was in vain. When the Legislature met in the winter of 1879, Mr. Seitz introduced S. B. No. 221, to cover Mr. Foster's case, and to "Preserve the Purity of Elections." The bill attracted public attention. It was carefully considered, and thoroughly debated in both houses, and some startling statements were made as to the corrupt use of money by Mr. Foster. It was generally understood that the proposed law was intended to cover Mr. Foster's case, and, if possible, prevent others from following in his footsteps. This bill became a law, and is now a part of our Revised Statutes, as follows:

SEC. 7064. Whoever, being a candidate for an office of trust or profit under the constitution or laws of this state, or of the United States, loans, or directly or indirectly gives or offers or promises to give, any money or other thing of value, to any elector within the district in which he is a candidate, for the purpose of influencing or retaining the vote of such elector, or to any person to secure or retain the influence of such person in his behalf as such candidate, or to be used by such person to influence the vote of any elector, or of electors generally, or to influence him or them to vote or to refrain from voting, shall be fined not more than one thousand and not less than five hundred dollars, or imprisoned in the penitentiary not more than three years, and be forever ineligible to any office of trust or profit within this state; and a violation of any provision of this section, by any person elected to any such office, shall render his election void, and, if he has taken office, shall operate as a vacation of the same; but this section shall not be construed to apply to hospitality extended at the residence of such candidate.

SEC. 7065. Whoever, not being a candidate for office, disburses, or gives, or promises to give, any money, or other thing of value, or gives or treats to any spirituous, malt, or other liquors, directly or indirectly to influence an elector in giving or withhold ing his vote, or, with intent to induce him to vote contrary to his inclinations, seeks by violence or threats to enforce the payment of a debt, or to begin a criminal prosecution, or to injure the business or trade of an elector; or, if an employer of laborers, or an agent of such employer, threatens to withhold or reduce the wages of, or to dismiss from service, any laborer in his employ, or refuses to allow to any such employe the time to attend at the place of election and vote; or whoever sells or offers to sell his influence with electors for a valuable consideration, or with, or by means of anything of value, seeks to influence the vote of an elector, or to influence him to vote, or refrain from voting, shall be fined not more than two thousand nor less than one hundred dollars, or imprisoned in the penitentiary not more than three years.

SEC. 7066. Whoever asks, demands, or receives of a candidate for nomination to any office by a political party or convention, or of a candidate for an office under any law, any money, or anything of value, not then due and owing, or makes application to any such candidate to purchase a ticket to, or to give any money or any other thing of value for any pretended ball, pic-nic, fair, entertainment or charitable enterprise, with the expectation or belief that such demand, request, or receipt will influence the vote of an elector, shall be fined not more than three hundred nor less than fifty dollars, or imprisoned sixty days in the county jail, or a workhouse, if there is such an institution in the county, or be both fined and imprisoned; and such demand or request of a candidate shall be deemed *prima facie* evidence of such expectation or belief; but prosecutions under this and the two preceding sections must be commenced within six months after the commission of the act complained of.

VII. This law had no terrors for Mr. Foster. No one has ever been arrested or convicted under its provisions. No one ever will be, as long as the one who asks, takes or receives, is punished for doing so. Before the law was in print, Mr. Foster's agents were covering the state in his interests, and securing pledges for support, and arranging to capture delegates to the state convention.

Greenbacks were on a par with gold and silver. Resumption, proposed in 1875, was a fact. There was a general revival of business, the credit for which was equally divided between Hon. John Sherman and the Republican party.

Mr. Sherman was serving as Secretary of the Treasury under Mr. Hayes. A fortunate combination of circumstances had enabled him as an executive officer to carry out the financial plans he had favored as a legislator. His name was freely used as a candidate for Governor, but not with his consent. He wanted to be President, and he fondly hoped that the success of resumption, the return of prosperity, and his long identity with the financial measures of the Republican party would point toward Mr. Sherman as the logical candidate. He did not think it would comport with his career, or the dignity of his position as a cabinet officer, to make the race for Governor of Ohio. But the selection in 1876 of the Governor of Ohio as the candidate of one party, and the Governor of New York as the candidate of another, had made a fashion that politicians were willing to follow. Mr. Foster's ambitions had grown and expanded into great proportions in the nine years since he had left the honest and modest paths and by-ways of a useful commercial life. He knew that there were great possibilities in the future and the office of Governor. He wanted it, and when Mr. Foster wanted anything in Ohio politics, if money could persuade it to roost under his vine and fig tree, it was persuaded. Mr. Hayes and his administration were grateful to Mr. Foster for the services he had rendered at a critical time, and the cordial support he had given both. It was natural that Mr. Foster should have the support of both. But the Stalwarts were opposed to Mr. Foster to a man, for reasons given or implied in the statements made in this chapter. They favored Judge Alphonso Taft, whom Mr. Foster had so shrewdly flanked in 1875 and supplanted by R. B. Hayes.

One of Mr. Foster's aids and managers in this contest was Alex. Sands, sometimes known as "Big Six" and "The Archbishop." These titles had been given him by the thoughtless and innocent, because of Mr. Sands' usefulness and suavity in his political labors. He made a specialty of politics and was a successful "Boss" in his day and generation. He had the valuable aid and co-operation of his friend, Hon. Benjamin Eggleston, and a newspaper, *The*

Cincinnati Times. Mr. Sands did not confine his efforts to any particular party, candidate, cause or locality within the bounds of Ohio, but provided with the resources, he could make himself useful to any one who cared to charter his valuable services. His newspaper was never a part of the bargain. It was always thrown in for good measure and as a guarantee of good faith. The Republican State Central Committee fixed the meeting of the convention for the latter part of May, and it was to be held in Cincinnati. This being Judge Taft's home, it was considered a great victory for him, and his nomination was looked upon as a foregone conclusion. But Mr. Foster had never spread himself over the whole state before, and they did not know his "capacity for organization."

On May 22d, a week before the convention convened, a correspondent wrote from Columbus to the *Cincinnati Gazette*, that out of 149 delegates chosen in 19 Republican counties, 105 were outspoken for Taft and 44 were for Foster. There were 51 delegates from Hamilton County, and of these Mr. Foster secured 12, much to the surprise of Mr. Taft's friends and to the content of Mr. Sands' mind. This defection in Mr. Taft's own county made it easier to secure delegates that were wavering, as it was a conclusive argument that Mr. Taft was unpopular at home. It was a strong reason for inducing the delegates from the back counties to change their minds when a cash consideration was offered. The convention met in Music Hall. It was a large and demonstrative gathering. Mr. Sands, with considerate foresight, had provided a considerable number of enthusiastic patriots, who made a large amount of noise at opportune times, in favor of Mr. Foster, and upon any statement that could in any way have a reference to him. Being the home of Mr. Taft these demonstrations had no small weight with the heedless and innocent delegate. Mr. Sands fully approved Mr. Blaine's statement that "the power of the mob in controlling public opinion, is immeasurable. In monarchical governments it has dethroned kings, and in republics it dictates candidates."

Wm. Dennison presided over the convention. Many of the prominent men of the party were delegates. The secretary was Wm. Leonard, of Cleveland, a useful man with a lead pencil, and one that could be relied upon to make the proper additions on the side of his sympathies. There were only two candidates presented to the convention and balloted for, Mr. Foster and Mr. Taft. A ballot was taken, and the president of the convention announced that 565 votes had been cast, and that the secretary would announce the result. It was thought by all who had followed the vote closely that Mr. Taft had an undoubted majority, but there was unnecessary delay at the table of the secretaries, and when the chairman made his announcement,

Mr. W. D. Bickham, of the *Dayton Journal*, challenged the vote. He called the attention of the convention to the fact that there was only 554 votes in the convention, and the secretary had reported 12 more votes than there were votes in the convention. Mr. Dennison grasped the situation and quickly said that if this was the case he would order another ballot. This declaration created great consternation among the Foster managers. Another ballot meant the overwhelming defeat of their favorite, for they had unmasked their forces, and could not rally them. They had not foreseen and provided for such an unexpected emergency.

The fatal blunder of the secretary was speedily corrected. In his eagerness and hilarity he had anticipated Mr. Foster's victory and had overdone his task. The chairman, after some pressure, blandly announced that the secretary had corrected the slight error in his figures (by striking off 12 votes), and he would announce the result. He declared that Mr. Foster had received $280\frac{1}{6}$ votes; Mr. Taft $272\frac{5}{6}$ votes and Mr. Kiefer 2 votes. It required 279 votes to nominate. Mr. Foster was duly declared the regular nominee, amidst the applause of Mr. Sands' friends in the galleries and the curses and angry denunciations of Mr. Taft's friends on the floor. Mr. Benjaman Eggleston, as a friend of Mr. Taft (in disguise), promptly moved that Mr. Foster's nomination be made unanimous, and the motion was carried, and

Mr. Foster was escorted to the hall and proceeded to read a speech from manuscript telling how highly he felt honored at being so unexpectedly chosen. There was an element of the ridiculous in the situation. Many delegates and most of the audience left the hall while Mr. Foster was reading his speech. There was loud complaint and much indignation over the awarding of the prize to Mr. Foster, and the corrupt and unfair methods used to defeat Mr. Taft.

A canvass of the delegates the night before the convention showed Taft had 314 votes, Foster 227, with a few votes scattering. An instance that can be proven by ample testimony, will show how Mr. Foster secured the nomination. Noble County had three delegates in the convention. The delegation was headed by Hon. James Dalzell, known as "Private Dalzell." He is a country lawyer of some influence and a limited practice in his profession. He served two terms in the Legislature, and attained his notoriety by numerous cards in the public prints, putting down the War of the Rebellion. An examination of his record as a soldier shows that when his regiment was preparing for battle, sickness conveniently called Mr. Dalzell to the rear, and he has killed more rebels since the war than he did during actual hostilities. When Mr. Dalzell arrived in Cincinnati to attend Mr. Foster's convention, he secured a cot at a hotel, in the room of the Athens delegation. Mr. Taft had no louder nor warmer advocate among the great crowd than Mr. Dalzell was the night before the convention. When the roll call began it was seen that the contest would be close; a delegate from Athens went to the Noble delegation and asked how they stood. "Solid for Taft," was Mr. Dalzell's ready reply. Before the delegate could regain his seat Noble County was called, and Mr. Dalzell stood on a chair and announced, "Noble County casts her three votes for Charles Foster!" This unexpected announcement and the astonishing change in Guernesy and other counties showed that a number of Taft delegates had been seduced.

After the convention adjourned Mr. Dalzell met several of the Athens delegation in their room, and one of them denounced him as an infamous scoundrel, and ordered him to seize his carpet-sack and vacate the room. Mr. Dalzell pleaded with the justly indignant Taft man and said, "You must not be too hard on us. You know we are poor up in Noble, and one of Mr. Foster's agents paid our railroad fare and our hotel bill." "Is this *all* you got? Why didn't you come to your friends; they would have done as much, and while you were selling out, why in the hell didn't you sell yourselves for something?" It is probable that Mr. Dalzell's well-known modesty restrained him from making known the precise sum he received for the votes from Noble County.

The Democrats nominated a soldier ticket, Gen.

Thomas Ewing for Governor and Gen. A. V. Rice for Lieutenant-Governor. Mr. Ewing could not stem the tide of rising prosperity. He made a splendid canvass, but received no financial help from any source. He was embarrassed in the midst of his canvass by the treachery of one who held an important place upon the campaign committee. Mr. Carson Lake, of Akron, a newspaper man, was secretary of the executive committee, and as such was selling or giving the secrets of the organization to the Cleveland *Leader*. Aided by his own and the Democratic committee, Mr. Foster was elected by the largest majority the Republicans had carried Ohio by since 1872. The largest total vote (669,159) was cast that had ever been polled in the history of the state. Mr. Foster received 336,261; Mr. Ewing, 319,132; Mr. Gideon T. Stewart, 4,145; Mr. A. Sanders Piatt, 9,072, and Mr. John Hood, 547. The Republican Legislature chosen with Mr. Foster, elected James A. Garfield United States Senator. With his inauguration as Governor of Ohio, Mr. Foster reached the zenith of his life. He aided others to higher preferment but could not help himself.

COL. CALVIN $ELLERS BRICE.

"THERE'S MILLIONS IN IT."

(*Porcupine, Nov. 1889.*)

CHAPTER VII.

THE DISGRACEFUL SCRAMBLE FOR THE OHIO DELEGATION IN 1880.—THURMAN, PAYNE AND JEWETT.

There are, thank heaven,
A nobler troop to whom this trust is given,
Who, all unbribed, at Freedom's altar stand
Faithful and firm, bright warders of the land!
By them still lifts the press its arm abroad
To guide all curious men along life's road,
To cheer young Genius; Pity's tear to start,
In truth's bold cause to rouse each fearless heart,
To hunt corruption from his secret den,
And show the master up, the gaze of wondering men.
—*Sprague's Curiosity.*

PLUTARCH, in his immortal *Lives* of the few that have escaped the oblivion that has overtaken the multitudes, tells a stately story of Cato, the Younger. He had a brother, Cæpio, to whom he was deeply attached. The loss of their parents had bound the orphans stronger in the sincere ties of happy brotherhood. When but a child, Cato was asked whom he loved most, and his answer was, "my brother." He was then asked whom he loved next to his brother, and his answer was, "my brother." When the brothers reached manhood, Cato went as an officer to Macedonic and commanded a legion under Rubrius. His brother was stationed at Ænus, in Thrace. Word reached Cato that Cæpio was very sick, and he put to sea, from Thessalonica, in a small boat, with several friends and slaves, and after a narrow escape from wreck and drowning, they arrived at Ænus, just after Cæpio had expired. Cato showed the sensibility of a brother, rather than the fortitude of a philosopher. He wept, he groaned, he embraced the dead body, and, besides these and other tokens of the greatest sorrow, he spent vast sums upon the funeral. The spices and rich robes that were burned with the body, were very expensive, and he erected a monument for him of Thasian marble in the forum at Ænus, which cost no less than eight talents. The lavish expenditure of money, and display of wealth and magnificence, at his brother's funeral, excited great comment at Rome, both favorable and antagonistic, and many condemned Cato, because of his severe simplicity, extreme opposition and rugged hostility to the prevalent luxury and corrupt tendencies of his age and people. Although among the richest men of Rome, his economical habits and opposition to the extravagance of the wealthy classes, led many to believe that he was miserly and parsimonious and loved money, rather than simplicity. He courageously exposed and attacked the corrupt practices and ambitious purposes of Julius Cæsar, and the latter assailed him in a work known as *The Anti-Cato*. In this Julius Cæsar alludes to the incident of the funeral of Cato's brother, and to belittle his character before the people, he charges, that Cato passed the ashes of his brother and of the funeral pile through a sieve, to recover anything of value that might have been melted by the flames.—We are sifting the ashes of dead events, in our political life, to discover the truth.

II. The inauguration of Charles Foster as Governor of Ohio, the election of James A. Garfield to the United States Senate, although still a member of the House of Representatives, and the endorsement of John Sherman as a favorite son, and as the candidate of the Ohio Republicans for the Presidency, were events that followed fast upon each other's heels, in the early part of 1880. Ex-President Grant had spent several years abroad, as the honored guest of many nations, rulers and people. His return to his own country, whether accidental or designed, was upon the eve of the Presidential election. The receptions tendered him in the leading cities, were the result of the sincere regard felt for him by the people. His absence from his own country, had quieted the tongues of partisan malice, and the apprehension and jealousy of political rivals. The people were anxious and willing to welcome home and do honor to a man that had been a successful commander of their armies and twice held the highest office in their gift.

Grant's party and political friends were not slow to take advantage of this popular favor, and use it to aid in the accomplishment of their immediate political ambitions. His former friends and political allies feared the magic of James G. Blaine's name, and his nomination by the Republican convention seemed an almost foregone conclusion, until the return of their idol.

It was charged that the Ex-President was again a candidate for a third term. He neither affirmed nor denied this charge. He did not restrain the enthusiasm of his friends. His attitude aroused all the fears that existed during his second term in office. Former charges were renewed with greater emphasis and more embittered feeling. The Republican party now entered upon the fiercest factional fight that the organization had ever known. The Republican National Convention met in Chicago, the first week of June, 1880. The Ohio delegation was headed by such well known men as Ex-Gov. Dennison, James A. Garfield, Gov. Foster and Benj. Butterworth. In numbers, the delegation was for John Sherman, at heart, it was against him. On the preliminary questions, such as the unit rule, which divided the convention, the Ohio delegation was about equally divided, and this lack of unity destroyed all of its influence as far as Mr. Sherman was concerned. His enemies within his own party, and from his own state, were bold and bitter in their attacks. It was duly charged against Mr. Sherman and other candidates that the Negro delegates from the South had been bought up, but the trouble with the colored brother was that he would not remain purchased long enough for the goods to be located and the votes counted. Among the specific charges made by Charles Moore, of Columbus, afterwards one of Gov. Foster's appointees, was, that a check for $100 had been given Reuben L. Smith, a colored delegate from Florida, and a railroad ticket from Washington City to Chicago and return. The check was in Mr. Sherman's handwriting, and it was charged that it and the ticket had been given Mr. Smith by Mr. Sherman for his vote; but as Mr. Smith's vote was cast with the vote of Florida, for Mr. Grant, and was one of the immortal 306, these charges may be considered as having been made but not proven. The check and Mr. Smith were both photographed for future use. The attitude of Ohio Republicans had a demoralizing effect upon the Ohio delegation, which contained at least two ambitious men, and many others on the delegation who were obeying the plain letter of their instructions, but violating the spirit, if the instructions ever had a Sherman soul. The attitude of Ohio delegations, in National Conventions of both parties for many years, has not been creditable to either party, and has fallen short of reflecting honor upon the state. Upon this occasion, both Gov. Foster and Mr. Garfield must be credited with commendable state pride. If either one of them could not get first or second place on the ticket, they were in favor of Mr. Sherman for whatever he could get. These two made studied and dramatic entrances at conveniently arranged periods, into the hall, and by the most fortunate combination of circumstances and a judicious distribution of tickets, that seemed fore-ordained, there was always a body of patriots that were blind to the presence of any one in that historical gathering but Foster and Garfield, and they never made their appearance upon the scene without a boisterous welcome that bordered upon popularity, and attracted all eyes to these Siamese twins from Ohio. This by-play, so successful on this occasion, has been imitated since by other sons of Ohio, but without such gratifying results.

The convention continued a week, and ran over Sunday. There seemed to be a determination to starve the Southern brothers of both colors, into submission. On Saturday night the grandest oratorical display, to the greatest audience that America had ever seen, took place. Roscoe Conkling presented the name of the illustrious Grant, and James A. Garfield placed himself in nomination, under the guise of presenting the name of John Sherman of Ohio. If Blaine should be nominated, Gov. Foster was playing for second place. If Garfield could be nominated, Gov. Foster was willing to be looked upon as his Creator. Mr. Garfield was nominated. His nomination was chiefly due to the management of Gov. Foster and the timely action of the Indiana delegation, led by Benj. Harrison.

The old Guard did not surrender. On the 36th and last ballot, Garfield had 399 votes, Grant 306, Blaine 42, Washburn 5, and Ohio's favorite son John Sherman 3. Out of the five candidates at the finish, three of them were Ohio's sons, and it was natural that one of these should win the prize. But the general opinion was, that the wrong son had won, and this view was sustained by both the friends of Grant and Sherman.

III. The unexpected result of the Republican convention, and the angry protests of the partisans of the defeated candidates, filled the Democrats with great hopes. Garfield was a local man in Ohio. He had never been a candidate before the people of the state for any office. There was a general impression that he had secured his own nomination by being false to his state, her instructions and the anointed choice of his party in Ohio. Sam'l J. Tilden would like to have been vindicated, by a nomination as the Democratic candidate, but his age, his health and the exposures of corrupt proposals by his friends and those bound to him by ties of blood and interest, in the "Fraud of 1876," made it impolitic to put him at the head of the Democratic column. Before the convention convened, it was generally understood that he would not be a candidate, and there was a well founded rumor that Henry B. Payne, of Ohio, had been named as Mr. Tilden's heir. But one of "the people from the Southward," was in the field. At the convention of

Ohio Democrats, held the first week in May, at Columbus, Allen G. Thurman had been unanimously endorsed, as their first choice for the nomination for President, and no other name had been mentioned. The delegation to the national convention which was to meet in Cincinnati in June, had been *requested* to give their united support to Mr. Thurman. Hugh J. Jewett's name was mentioned as a candidate under certain conditions. Again "one of the people to the Southward," was in opposition to one of New England birth and lineage. Allen G. Thurman was opposed by Henry B. Payne.

There is a thread of romance, an element of sentiment, a purpose, and a providence running all through the political events of Ohio, as there has been in other affairs of the state. How narrow and restricted human foresight is, when it attempts to pierce the veil of the future. Rev. Manasseh Cutler, anxious for the welfare of the State that he and his associates were about to found, did not think "the people to the Southward," were desirable as companions in the new venture. In his own lifetime they so dominated and controlled the destinies of the new state, that Mr. Cutler, as a member of Congress, voted to prevent Ohio from entering the Union. In the continued conflict of years, since Ohio became a state, "the people to the Southward" have worthily borne the burdens of all our struggles, and have reflected honor upon the growing glory of Ohio. It is the sons of

New England, the descendants of the Puritans, your Paynes, your Fosters, and your Brices, that have yielded to the temptations of wealth, and have corrupted the people. "The people to the Southward," your Allens, your Thurmans, and your Durbin Wards, have ever stood against corrupt men and methods, in battling for the preservation of free institutions and upholding the rights of the people.

Allen G. Thurman's humble birth, useful life, and honorable career has laid to rest the prevalent "13" superstition. He was born in Lynchburg, Va., Nov. 13, 1813. His father was a preacher, too, and died when he was a child, after the family had removed to Chillicothe O., in 1821. His mother was a sister of Wm. Allen, and to her watchful care Mr. Thurman acknowledges that he owes the bent and habits that formed his character and mind. In 1878, in debate, in reply to an attack by Mr. Blaine, in the Senate, Mr. Thurman began his speech by saying: "I was born a plain country lawyer," but the records show that notwithstanding this fact, as stated by Mr. Thurman, he studied law, and was admitted to the bar and began the practice of law in 1835. In 1844 he married Mary Dun, of Kentucky, and the same year he was elected to Congress, at the election of James K. Polk, President.

In 1851 he was elected a Judge of the Supreme Court of Ohio, and served until 1856. In 1867 he ran for Governor, was beaten, and was elected to the

United States Senate. In 1873, his uncle, Wm. Allen, was elected Governor, with a Democratic Legislature, which elected Mr. Thurman to a second term in the United States Senate. In 1880, Mr. Thurman was approaching the close of his twelve years service in Congress. He was in his 67th year. The Presidency was an honor which his life and public services had qualified him to fill, and gave him no small claim upon the consideration of his party, if great merit and faithful services are qualifications. His unanimous and apparently hearty endorsement by his party in Ohio was a gratifying evidence of his high standing at home, but the attacks of the Cincinnati *Enquirer*, and the persistent opposition of Washington and John McLean, weakened Mr. Thurman as a candidate, and prepared the way for the Bosses and Boodle to debauch the Ohio delegation, and bring shame upon the state and disgrace upon the Ohio Democracy. It is an unfortunate habit of the Ohio Democrats to denounce the corrupt practices of the Republicans one year, and proceed to indulge in the same evils the next. The example has been fatally contagious. The fact that the National Convention was to be held in Cincinnati, and other causes, formed a combination favorable to an Ohio man, and the logic of events pointed to Mr. Thurman as that man. But alas, Mr. Thurman had no "bar'l," and above all, he was averse to the corrupt expenditure of money in politics. Unfortunately there were Democrats who did have money, and whose friends were heartily in favor of using it in any manner to attain a desired end. Among those who were brought forward as candidates for the great prize, were Hugh J. Jewett and Henry B. Payne. When the State Convention met their names were not mentioned, except quietly, and no effort was made to influence the delegates or the convention. But as the delegates were chosen by districts, before or after the State Convention convened, the agents and partisans of both these candidates labored to secure the selection of men favorable to their favorites.

IV. Hugh J. Jewett had resigned his seat in Congress from the Franklin district in 1874, and had removed to New York City, to accept the receivership of the Erie Railroad. He was "one of the people to the Southward," having been born in Hartford Co., Maryland, about 1815. He began practicing law in 1838, and in 1840 he located in St. Clairsville, Belmont County, O., and in 1848 he removed to Zanesville. He confined his practice to those questions involving financial problems, and became a very successful corporation lawyer. In 1852 he was made president of the Muskingum branch of the Ohio Bank. In 1853 he was elected to the State Senate, and was appointed United States District Attorney. He became interested in railroad enterprises, and in 1857 he was elected President of the Central Ohio Railroad, now a part of the Baltimore & Ohio system, and later he held a similar place on the Little Miami and Muskingum Valley roads, and was a Vice-President of the P. S. & St. L. Railroad. In 1861 he was the Democratic candidate for Governor, and was defeated by David Tod, the Union candidate. He was a candidate for United States Senator in 1863, but the Democrats were in a minority in the Legislature. In 1867 he was elected to the State Senate and helped elect Allen G. Thurman to the United States Senate. Mr. Jewett was a Democrat by birth, but not by occupation. His life, business and associates do not constitute the soil which is congenial to the growth of Democratic principles His capacity for managing great financial interests, and untangling complicated business affairs, was of the highest order. It was unfortunate for his fame, that either by himself or others, he permitted the use of large sums of money to further his candidacy for the Democratic nomination for the Presidency. It brought nothing but dishonor to a name hitherto unsullied, and put a weight upon a name and character, that otherwise might have passed into history with a just renown.

By the use of money, Mr. Jewett's friends did not advance his interests, but they helped destroy the character and influence of the Ohio delegation, and made it utterly impossible for Allen G. Thurman, or any other Ohio man to secure the nomination.

V. Henry B. Payne, of Cleveland, O., was born in Hamilton, Madison County, N. Y., Nov. 30, 1810.

His family came from Connecticut. His mother was a Douglas, and he and Stephen A. Douglas were blood relations. He and Douglas studied law in the same town, and at the same time, and began a friendship that ended only with death. Douglas came to Cleveland in the winter of 1833, and was taken sick and nearly died. Three months later, Payne came to Cleveland and found Douglas in a bad condition, and nursed him back to health. Douglas at once left Cleveland in disgust, and went to Illinois. Payne having divided his fortune, $100, with his friend. A year later young Payne began the practice of law in Cleveland, but in 1846 he abandoned his profession on account of ill health. His tastes inclined toward business, and he early discerned the fact that Cleveland was destined to be a great city. He married Miss Perry, a daughter of Nathan Perry, one of the wealthiest men in the city. He invested liberally in every enterprise that he thought would help build up a great city. He took an active part in municipal affairs, and held many places. He was the first president of the Cleveland & Columbus Railroad, and was interested in all the railroads that now constitute the magnificent system that centers in Cleveland. In 1849 he was sent to the Ohio Legislature. In 1851 he became a member of the State Senate, and was a candidate for United States Senator against Benj. F. Wade, and was beaten by one vote. In 1857 he was the Democratic candidate for Governor, against Salmon P. Chase, and was beaten 1,503 votes. Chase received 160,568, Payne 159,065, and Van Tump 10,272.

It is said, but we do not vouch for the truth of the statement, that if Allen G. Thurman and "the people to the Southward," were jealous of Mr. Payne and his prominence in the party, and if they had not withheld their cordial support, he would have beaten Chase, and might have made great changes in history. Mr. Payne was an elector-at-large in the Cass campaign; he was a delegate to the National Conventions in 1856, 1860 and 1872. He and George H. Pugh led the fight at the Charleston Convention, and he made the minority report of the Committee on Resolutions, and replied to the attacks of Toombs and Yancey. He was the first man from the North in a generation that taught the "fire-eater" that there were some Democrats in the North who had rights and convictions that they would not surrender and did not fear to maintain. He foresaw that war would follow the disruption of the Democratic party at the Charleston Convention. When war came he did not abandon his party, but he favored the suppression of the Rebellion, and the preservation of the Union. In 1861, when Hugh J. Jewett ran for Governor, Mr. Payne was a candidate for Judge upon the ticket. In 1874 he was nominated for Congress, in Cleveland. In accepting the nomination, he said: "If elected, and my life is spared to serve out the term, I promise to come back with hand and heart as undefiled and clean as when I left you." He was elected but did not keep his word. He favored the Electoral Commission and served as a member of the "7," who could not out-vote the "8." He was a member of the House Committee on Banking and Currency, and prepared a plan of compromise on the currency that was adopted by a Democratic Caucus, after three months discussion, in which the paper advocates and gold men nearly disrupted the party. Like Mr. Thurman, Mr. Payne never departed from the sound and historic teachings of his party upon the money question. With the end of Mr. Payne's term in Congress in 1877, his public career ended for a time. He was mentioned as a candidate for the United States Senate against Geo. H. Pendleton, in 1878, but only received a few votes in the Democratic caucus. A campaign of a questionable character was made in which thousands of dollars were foolishly spent by ill-advised friends, and nothing accomplished except to place Mr. Payne's good name in jeopardy. It seems that a good name and great riches can not go hand in hand in public life, especially if a man is a father, like Mr. Payne and Mr. Jewett, and has sons who have money, like Oliver Payne and Geo. Jewett, who are not backward in spending it to promote a father's ambition and fame. But what a father can not earn by his abilities, merits and opportunities, the sons can not buy with money. There are offices for sale, but honor can not be bought.

VI. Mr. Payne had three children living at this time. A daughter had married Wm. C. Whitney of New York, and two sons, Nathan and Oliver, lived in Cleveland. Nathan Payne was a companionable and lovable fellow, with a great capacity for spending money, and little for its accumulation. He had a weakness for politics, and lost no opportunity, that he thought would advance his father's interests. Oliver Payne became identified with the Standard Oil Corporation, and was a large stockholder, and held an important official position in that great and powerful body. Politics had no charms for him. He was proud of his father's public career, and his sole and commendable purpose in life, was to see the long and useful career of a worthy sire, rounded out by further and greater honors. To accomplish this, Oliver Payne was willing to spend fabulous sums of money. This well known disposition was taken advantage of by politicians, and whenever there was a vacancy in any office, worthy of Henry B. Payne's high standing, and which it was thought he would consent to fill, an agitation was begun in the press, by such able engineers as Col. W. W. Armstrong of the Cleveland *Plain Dealer*, and it was made to appear that there was a popular demand for Mr. Henry B. Payne—an aching void that he alone could fill. There was also a private demand upon Mr. Oliver Payne's purse, which he promptly met, and liberally increased as occasion seemed to require and justify the use of money.

Henry B. Payne was not a candidate for the nomination for the Presidency. He knew how elusive this phantom had ever been. He knew how dangerous, if not dishonorable, it would be to have his name used after Allen G. Thurman had been so cordially endorsed by the Ohio Democracy. But under the leadership of W. W. Armstrong, David R. Paige and other ill-starred advisers, it was a Payne boom or "bust," and they "busted." But they secured the selfish object of their dark work. They induced Oliver Payne to make liberal expenditures of money.

After the New York State Democratic convention, Wm. C. Whitney, Mr. Payne's son-in-law, headed the delegation to the National convention, and when it was known that Mr. Payne could secure the solid vote from New York State, efforts were at once made to divide the Ohio delegation and drive Mr. Thurman from the field as a candidate. W. W. Armstrong and David R. Paige, at an early stage in the contest, had both visited New York City, and pledged their support to Hugh J. Jewett. They both took his money to aid his canvass. Later both as delegates to the national convention from their districts, declared in favor of Mr. Payne, and received and used money to aid his canvass. There is a magical touch in Boodle that enables the Bosses to perform some surprising acrobatic feats, and cut antics before high heaven that pass the comprehension of the ordinary mind. God may see and understand, men never can.

The Payne agents went over Ohio visiting the delegates, and trying by argument and money to secure their pledges to support Mr. Payne. Out of the 44 delegates, the Jewett men claimed 18, the Payne men 14, and this left 12 out of 44 delegates who had been instructed by a state convention for Allen G. Thurman, to carry his banner into the great contest. Mr. Thurman and his friends were not ignorant of what was going on. Telegrams and letters kept him advised of the movements of Mr. Payne's agents, but he did not know until too late of the trail of golden grease that these agents had left in various sections of the state. The operations of the Payne agents were not confined to Ohio. No effort was lost to convince the delegates in other states, that Mr. Thurman was not the choice of the Ohio Democracy, notwithstanding the action of the convention which had unanimously endorsed him. David R. Paige made a missionary tour to the West Virginia Democratic convention two weeks before the Cincinnati convention, and labored to secure the endorsement of that state for Mr. Payne, because he had a majority of the Ohio delegation and not Mr. Thurman. This was the manner in which the instructions of the Ohio Democrats were obeyed, "to use every honorable effort to secure the nomination of Allen G. Thurman."

VI. A final attempt was made by Mr. Thurman to check this treason and to turn back the rising tide of corruption. He sent out a letter to the members of the Ohio delegation, to meet him in conference at Columbus, O., on Saturday, June 18. Some twenty-one out of the forty-four responded to the call. Those present were: Gen. Jas. B. Steedman of Toledo, and Hon. Jno. McSweeney of Wooster, delegates at large; Geo. Hoadly, Chas. Baker, Alex. Long and Julius Reis of Cincinnati, all opposed to Thurman and eager to cut his political throat; W. J. Alexander of Spring Valley, Chas. Brosel of New Bremen, W. H. Hill of Defiance, L. T. Neal of Chillicothe, John G. Thompson of Columbus, Chas. D. Martin of Lancaster, John O. Neil of Tiffin, Henry Bohl of Marietta, C. C. Lewis of Caldwell, Frank Marriott of Delaware, Wm. E. Haynes of Fremont, S. Clements of Bucyrus, John Farley of Cleveland, David R. Paige of Akron, and D. L. Coleman of Ravenna. Most of these were Mr. Thurman's enemies and stood pledged to Mr. Payne or Mr. Jewett. It was a sad meeting. It reminded one of the vultures waiting on the fence for the horse to die, so that they could pick the bones. Senator Thurman, accompanied by Senator Pendleton, arrived from Washington, and went to the meeting. No one knew what the meeting had been called for. All were eager to learn. Geo. Hoadly, nervous and jerky, and always in a hurry, like a lawyer with more business than he could attend to, broke the ice and ended the suspense, by saying that they had gathered at the request of Mr. Thurman and were ready to hear from him. The venerable Senator said his name had been mentioned as a candidate for the nomination for the Presidency, but it was not his candidacy. He had been put forward as the candidate of Ohio, and he hoped every Democrat who went to Cincinnati, would go as an Ohio Democrat and not as a Thurman man. He had assurances of strong support from other states, if Ohio was a unit and cordial in his support. He thought the Ohio Democracy were entitled to some recognition. The Republicans had showered honors upon their sons from Ohio, where Ohio Democrats had been ignored. He did not want to appear egotistical, but he thought he could carry Ohio against Mr. Garfield.

The speech was coldly received. Mr. Thurman was throwing snow-balls into a vast furnace of corruption in full blast. Geo. H. Pendleton made an eloquent plea for a united support of Mr. Thurman by the Ohio delegation. He was received in silence. W. D. Hill, of Defiance, threw diplomacy off, and denounced the attempts to weaken the influence of the Ohio delegation by saying it was not for Mr. Thurman. No other delegate said a word. Most of them sat like conspirators, conscious of their guilt. Judge Hoadly said he had to catch a train, and he moved that the delegation meet in Cincinnati, at the Grand Hotel, at 10 o'clock Monday. This was in accordance with the program cut and dried beforehand. Henry Bohl seconded the motion and it was put and carried, and the meeting passed into history as a pitiable spectacle of men being pleaded with to keep faith, and preserve their honor by obeying the instructions of the power that created them as delegates.

It took a large sum of the money of both Mr. Payne and Mr. Jewett to bring about this condition of affairs. When men are guilty of such open perfidy, there must be ample rewards to tempt them to such shameful conduct. Some men sold twice. Some had Mr. Jewett's money and took Mr. Payne's, and some ended by taking the money from both, and betraying all.

VII. The scene now shifts to Cincinnati. The forces from Ohio began gathering there on Sunday, June 19. The Payne managers were early on the ground, taking the shroud off of the corpse of the Thurman boom, and showing the remains eagerly to all who cared to gaze upon them. Among the men engaged in this occupation were W. W. Armstrong and John Farley, of Cleveland, and the brothers, Ralph and Dave Paige. The Thurman forces were led by Judge Bingham, of Columbus, O., and at a conference the Payne men were bitterly denounced for their treachery and attacks upon Mr. Thurman. This conflict among Ohio people, presented the state and the Democracy in a humiliating manner to the delegates and people from other states. The Payne agents had, by purchase and otherwise, secured a majority of the Ohio delegation, and under the unit rule, they claimed Ohio would be solid. The Cincinnati *Enquirer* lost no opportunity to abuse Thurman and belittle his candidacy. The object was revenge, not revenue. The Ohio delegation met at 10 o'clock Monday morning. Durbin Ward, the friend of Mr. Thurman, was presented for the chairmanship of the delegation. He was beaten by Alex. Long. The Thurman men had 20 votes, and the Payne men had 24. W. W. Armstrong was elected as a member of the National Committee vice John G. Thompson. To secure this place, Mr. Thompson had wavered in his support of Mr. Thurman, who had been his life-long friend. The very air reeked with treason and ingratitude. Boodle! Boodle!! Boodle!!! was everywhere dominant, and the Bosses were hilarious. Elated by their success in the morning, the Payne agents called a meeting of the delegation at 4 o'clock, Monday afternoon, and the animals got loose. The meeting was a stormy one; a resolution was offered and carried, that when a majority of the delegation demanded a conference, it should withdraw to consult and cast the solid vote for the one receiving a majority of the votes, which meant Mr. Payne. The adoption of this resolution brought on the long pending storm. The restraints of decency and reason had led the discordant elements in the delegation to treat each other with ordinary courtesy, but all these were thrown to the wind. Bribery and treason were openly charged. Men glared at each other, and friends of a lifetime shook their fists and threatened personal violence. No one will ever know the full particulars of that meeting. The participants by a common consent have been silent. Those that were boldest and bitterest in denunciation, did not care to repeat their language and charges in their calmer moments, and those who had been so freely charged with selling themselves, could not be expected to publish their own shame.

Those who were loyal to their party instructions and faithful in their support of Mr. Thurman were: Durbin Ward, Jas. B. Steedman, John McSweeney, M. H. Daniels, James E. Neal, J. V. Campbell, W. D. Hill, W. S. Alexander, Charles Boesel, E. D. Potter, W. W. Elsberry, L. T. Neal, S. J. Packard, W. H. Dugdale, Shannon Clements, Jas. W. Newman, John G. Thompson, Chas. D. Martin, John O. Neil, and J. H. Barrett.

Those who defied the instructions of the Ohio Democracy, for reason by some and consideration by others, supported Henry B. Payne, were: J. H. Wade, Geo. Hoadly, Alex. Long, Julius Reis, Charles Baker, John H. Farley, Jno. W. Nelson, F. B. Marriott, Jno. D. Thompson, W. E. Haynes, Geo. W. Roberts, G. J. Kenney, Jos. Ailshire, Henry Bohl, John Schiever, Dan. McConville, C. C. Lewis, R. S. Shields, C. N. Smick, D. R. Paige, D. S. Coleman, and W. W. Armstrong. The action of the delegation was made public and was used to influence New York and other delegations in favor of Mr. Payne.

VIII. The Thurman men were indignant and discouraged. A meeting was called on Monday night at Melodeon Hall to protest. It was a large and earnest gathering. Judge Jacob Meuser, of Crawford, presided. Hon. Geo. H. Pendleton sent a letter and recommended the adoption of the following:

"*Resolved:* That the candidacy of any citizen of Ohio, other than Allen G. Thurman, for the nomination for President, in advance of the presentation of his name to the convention, is repudiated by the Ohio Democracy, and is denounced as an act untrue to the will of the party as unanimously expressed in convention assembled."

Poor Pendleton. Little did he know, that three years later he was to pay for his temerity in supporting Thurman, by falling a victim to the same men, the same methods, and the Boodle from the same source, as had ended Allen G. Thurman's political life, and humiliated the Ohio Democracy. Gen. A. J. Warner spoke first. He read the resolutions adopted at Columbus by the state convention, declaring for Allen G. Thurman. He was Ohio's choice and was entitled to the *honest* support of every delegate. Judge Lincoln, of London, asked, if the delegates were honest, why had Durbin Ward been set aside, and Alex. Long, a pronounced enemy of Mr. Thurman, chosen as chairman of the delegation. He said

(23) delegates had signed a paper in favor of another candidate. He was afraid the Democrats had been betrayed at Columbus and were being betrayed at Cincinnati. Judge Samuel Hunter of Newark, said he was a native of Ohio, and never before had he had occasion to blush for his state. In every delegation where he had pleaded the cause of Mr. Thurman, he had been met with a sneer. There was treachery. Henry B. Payne did not dare be a candidate at Columbus, and should not be one now. No delegate could have been chosen had he proclaimed that he had a second choice, as he was doing here. He called upon the delegation to save the honor of Ohio and of the Democracy of the state. Frank McKinney, of Piqua, thought Allen G. Thurman was the biggest brained man in the world. He hoped the charges against the delegates were not well founded. Geo. L. Converse, of Columbus, made an oily gammon speech, to allay the rising indignation and divert the meeting from its purposes. Allen O. Myers said he had come from the Chicago convention, where he saw an Ohio man slaughtered by the treachery of the Ohio delegation. The act was being repeated here. The lesson was being taught that the way to political preferment lay through political treachery. Thurman's hands were clean, but he had no bar'l. Gen. J. B. Steedman, Judge Oliver and others spoke in a similar strain.

The Ohio delegation had another disgraceful meeting at night, and Durbin Ward and W. D. Hill made savage and severe charges against Geo. Hoadly. Thurman was dead, but his friends were fighting for the corpse, and were determined it should have decent burial, and be accompanied by victims, to appease his angry manes. The Payne men claimed 27 votes out of the Ohio delegation. The New York delegation wanted to know how long Ohio would support Thurman. Judge Hoadly and Alex. Long were sent to convey this important information, but the air was so lurid that they could not answer. Judge Hoadly was chosen temporary chairman of the convention. The first day of the convention was taken up with preliminary work. Gov. Stevenson, of Kentucky, was made permanent chairman of the convention. He was to have presented Mr. Thurman's name, but this task now devolved upon John McSweeney. A test ballot was taken the first day and resulted as follows: Hancock 171, Bayard 153½, Payne 81, Thurman 68½, Field 65, Morrison 62, Hendricks 49½, Tilden 38, and a few scattering votes.

The dissensions in the Ohio delegation were equalled by those in New York and Pennsylvania. The foxy manipulations of the sage of Gramercy Park were evident. He was muddying the waters, and hoped to catch the big fish himself. The balloting began on the second day. Gen. Hancock was the leading candidate. To kill him off the name of Samuel J. Randall was sprung at the last moment. But it was too late. The roll call was begun, and as it proceeded

Gen. Hancock's nomination seemed certain. An attempt was made to stem the tide, and turn it toward Randall by the Tilden forces, but it was futile. When Ohio was called, the delegation confirmed all stories of baseness that had been circulated, and they completed the humiliation of the Ohio Democracy, by asking leave to withdraw for consultation. A delegation that had been instructed to "use all honorable efforts to secure the nomination of Allen G. Thurman," ask permission to go out and see if they should vote for him! When the delegation returned, the vote was cast for Hancock, who had already been nominated. The final scene made the Ohio delegation absolutely ridiculous. The balloting for Vice-President was begun at once. The name of Gov. R. M. Bishop had been presented as a candidate for the nomination for Vice-President. The Ohio delegation withdrew again and by a vote of 17 to 16, agreed to support Durbin Ward instead of Gov. Bishop. While they were out, a member of the delegation, Dr. Ellsberry of Brown, arose and seconded the nomination of Wm. English, amidst great laughter and shouts of derision. The Ohio man was no longer the ringmaster of the political circus. Dressed in the motley of his own folly and misdeeds, he was the clown. When the delegation solemnly filed in, with Durbin Ward's tender unborn boom for Vice-President, the nomination of Wm. H. English, of Indiana, had been consummated.

THE TRIUMPHANT MARCH OF BOODLE.

(Porcupine, Jan. 1890.)

CHAPTER VIII.

BOOKWALTER'S BIG BAR'L.—THE CAMPAIGN OF 1881. CORRUPTION LIFTS ITS HEAD IN THE LEGISLATURE.— INDICTMENT OF MEMBERS AND A LOBBYIST FOR BRIBERY.

> The land wants such
> As dare with vigor execute the laws.
> Her festered sore must be lanced and linted.
> He's a bad surgeon that for pity spares
> The part corrupted till the gangrene spread,
> And all the body feverish. He that's merciful
> Unto the bad, is cruel to the good.
>
> *Randolph's Muse's Looking Glass.*

THE money expended in politics in Ohio, increased from year to year in an alarming manner. At a meeting of the Democratic State Central Committee, at Columbus, in the Spring of 1881, to fix the time and place for holding the State Convention, Mr. John G. Thompson, who had managed and mismanaged more political campaigns than any man in Ohio, made a speech in which he said: "We must have *grease* to run a campaign." In commenting upon this open declaration of Mr. Thompson, a correspondent of the Cincinnati *Enquirer*, in writing from Cleveland, said: "Mr. Thompson never had an idea in politics aside from the dollar. Experience has demonstrated that when the Ohio Democrats have the most money they do the worst. There is an element in the party that will not go near the polls unless they are paid, when they think there is money to be had; otherwise they go because they are Democrats. The Democrats can never raise money enough to buy an election in Ohio, and they can only win by poverty and an appeal to the patriotism of the people." Five thousand dollars use to be considered an ample sum to defray the legitimate expenses of a state campaign. Now this amount is not enough to conduct an ordinary campaign in one of the larger counties of the state. The liberality of Gov. Chas. Foster had revolutionized campaign methods, and provoked the agonizing lament of such practical politicians as Mr. Thompson. The expenses in ordinary campaigns fell chiefly upon the office-holders of both parties, and the demands of managers were becoming excessive and burdensome. As a result, these partisans were in favor of some innovation that would lift the burden from their shoulders and stop the drain from their pockets. Naturally they began to look for rich men in both parties as candidates who could be tickled with the prospects of political honors, and who were willing to part with a liberal portion of their wealth in payment for the same. It may be laid down as a rule, deducted from experience, that he who openly buys a nomination for any office, will be beaten for election. It is easy to purchase the politicians. The people are not for sale. The men who will sell in a convention, have their appetites whetted and must be bought again before an election. If this be so, it is a strong and conclusive argument in favor of the election of United States Senators by the people. That it is time, is made evident by the uniform opposition of the Senate to the proposed amendment to the Federal Constitution to bring about such a desirable reform. Our experience has demonstrated that while it is always safe to trust the people, it is never safe to trust the politicians, who are always the "Bosses and Boodlers" in our system.

II. The election of Mr. Garfield as President caused a readjustment by the Republican leaders of the party lines in Ohio. Mr. Sherman was very desirous of retaining his position as Secretary of the Treasury in Mr. Garfield's cabinet, and he made a strong bid for the place, but he was denied. Mr. Garfield owed his nomination to the Blaine men, and his election to the skillful but unfortunate truce that was patched up between the Grant and anti-Grant factions in the Republican party. It was soon evident that Mr. Garfield's administration was to be wholly under the domination of Mr. Blaine. In such a cabinet it would not be congenial to find a place for Mr. Sherman. Mr. Garfield was early confronted with the impossible task of reconciling the conflicting elements that raged around him, and in redeeming the promises made by him and for him at Chicago during the convention, and in Mentor before the election. But in the storm that he saw approaching but could not avert, even had he desired to do so, he saw the necessity of having, as far as possible, the support of a united party in his own state. To do this some provision had to be made for Mr. Sherman that would be acceptable to him and his large and faithful following in Ohio. Mr. Garfield held one office and had been elected to two others. His term in Congress expired in March, and he was to step from Congress to the White House. He resigned the senatorship in January, 1881, and Gov. Foster and his friends expected to secure this prize, but after consultation it was thought best to let Mr. Sherman return to his old place in the Senate, and Gov. Foster was promised a place in the cabinet. This would be a proper recognition of his services not only to his party but to Mr. Garfield, and the latter would have the benefit of the advice of a sage and sensible counselor to guide him between the extremes of conflicting interests as presented by the urgent demands of Mr. Blaine and his friends upon the one hand, and the imperious and haughty exactions of Roscoe Conklin upon the other. By this promotion, which he heartily desired and had every reason to expect, Mr. Foster would escape the burdens and large expense that must attend his second contest for Governor. As the time for the inauguration approached, Gov. Foster went to Washington, expecting to enter the new President's cabinet as Postmaster General.

Levi P. Morton, of New York, who had rendered valuable services at a critical period in the last Presidential campaign, by raising the money necessary to keep the wheels in motion, had been tendered and had accepted the tender of the Secretary of the Treasury. The appointment of Mr. Morton to this place was acceptable and satisfactory to Mr. Conklin and his friends in New York. But at the last moment, the experience of President Grant in nominating Mr. Stewart, the merchant prince of New York City, to the same office, was recalled. Congress in the latter case refused to repeal the law preventing one engaged in mercantile affairs from accepting this office, and the Senate refused to confirm the appointment and it was withdrawn. President Garfield sent for Mr. Morton and called his attention to the law, and said it would be impossible to appoint him. He induced Mr. Morton to accept the Secretaryship of the Navy. This change was the signal for the outbreak between the administration and Mr. Conklin and his friends, that led to the resignation of the latter and the assassination of the President. Mr. Morton conveyed the news of the change of program to Mr. Conklin, and it raised a great storm. It was taken as an evidence of bad faith upon the part of Mr. Garfield, and the act was laid at Mr. Blaine's door. Mr. Conklin held the ante-election pledge of Mr. Garfield as the price of his support that he should be consulted before any change or appointment was made in any office in New York. These facts were laid before Mr. Morton, and he felt that he could not, with honor and without betraying his friends, accept the Navy portfolio and he so notified the President. This disarranged the program and necessitated a hasty readjustment of the cabinet places. Again Mr. Foster was a victim to "the situation," and was asked to sacrifice himself and become a convenience for his friends. He did so. Mr. James of New York was made Postmaster General. Mr. Foster remained in Washington a month, trying to aid the President by his presence and advice, and returned to Ohio in April, when the war with Mr. Conklin was on. Mr. Foster came back thoroughly disgusted with politics. He was sick at heart, wounded in pride, wearied in mind, and ailing physically. This was his harvest after years of effort and the expenditure of a fortune in politics. He was a bankrupt in morals, and was soon to become one in money, but he was compelled to take up the contest in Ohio, and became the administration candidate for Governor. The convention met in Cleveland the first week in June. There were no candidates against Mr. Foster, but there was a great deal of opposition, and he was nominated by sufferance, and the shortest platform ever adopted by a Republican convention was agreed to. Mr. Garfield and Mr. Foster and the federal and state administrations were endorsed, and the convention adjourned after a lifeless session, that indicated serious party demoralization. The Republicans were greatly distressed over the serious conflict that had broken out between President Garfield and Senator Conklin.

III. The despondency among the Republicans, made the other end of the political teeter-board go up, and the Democrats were hopeful of carrying the state. The Washington end of the Ohio Democracy, as usual, wanted to dictate the policy of the party and name the candidate. They wanted a "Mossback" nominated upon a platform of National issues. The younger element of the party favored some one who could meet Charles Foster with money, and a campaign upon State issues. The Democratic State Central Committee met in May and called the State Convention to meet in Columbus on July 13. A number of Democrats of various degrees, ranging from prominent to obscure, were named in connection with the nomination for Governor. The number was so great as to be notable, and indicated the high hopes that burned in the bosom of Democracy. Col. C. W. Wooley, John F. Follett, Isaac Miller, Gen. H. B. Banning, Theodore Cook, of Cincinnati, W. W. Armstrong, of Cleveland, L. D. Thoman, of Youngstown, Judge Geo. W. Geddes, of Mansfield, Geo. Jewett, of Zanesville, Warren Noble, of Tiffin, and J. H. Thomas and John W. Bookwalter, of Springfield, were among those named as candidates. Mr. J. H. Thomas, for a time, seemed to be the most available candidate. Mr. Wm. C. Haynes, of Fremont, at the meeting of the State Central Committee had said: "That the Democracy want a candidate for Governor this year, who has no record, and who is so thoroughly unknown that it will take two weeks to find out who he is." The conflict among Ohio Democrats at the National Convention the year before, had called forth this remark. It would not be wise to take a candidate from either faction. Mr. Thomas seemed to fill the bill as to most of the requirements. Mr. Thomas studied law and devoted himself to business and manufacturing agricultural implements. He had prospered until he was looked upon as one of the wealthiest citizens of Springfield. He served for several years in the city council, and took a prominent and active interest in all that tended to advance the interests of the city. In 1868, he was the Democratic candidate for Congress, and came within 105 votes of defeating Mr. Winans, the Republican candidate. While in council, Mr. Thomas had voted in favor of an ordinance to close saloons at ten o'clock, and he believed in a "judicious license," to regulate the liquor traffic. The story was current that Mr. Thomas was a "crusader" and a "fanatic." This practically settled his availability as a candidate. He had been discovered as a candidate by Mr. D. C. Balantine, an editor and part owner of a paper called

"*The Transcript.*" Under his management, the paper frequently got the job and editorial departments mixed up. After earnestly advocating Mr. Thomas' candidacy for some time, the *Transcript's* zeal suddenly cooled, and the paper found another "favorite son" in the person of John W. Bookwalter, and it began a zealous advocacy of his candidacy for the Democratic nomination for Governor. Mr. Bookwalter was born near Hallville, Ross County, O., in 1837. His parents removed to Fountain County, Ind., and located on a farm. The boy got some schooling and plenty of hard work. He had a strong, original mind, and was a student, and his intellect early grappled with such mechanical problems, as the alarming waste of the forces of nature; the steam or mist arising from the waters that fell over a dam in the river near his father's farm, aroused his mind and led him to extended investigations. He went to Springfield as an uncouth and awkward country boy, and applied for a place to Mr. James Leffel, the manufacturer of the famous water wheel. Mr. Leffel was impressed by the strength and aptness of young Bookwalter's mind, and gave him employment. He proved faithful, industrious and competent. He grew in his employer's favor. He became his partner and married his daughter. He became wealthy, and when Mr. Leffel died he succeeded to his business.

Mr. Bookwalter had no political record. In fact his "politics" were so scarce that they were hard to locate. He had been a Republican but not a partisan. He left his party in the Greeley campaign. He had never had a strike in his shops. He was popular with his employes. In the Hancock campaign of 1880 he had carried a torch in a Democratic procession. He did this because it was charged that no man of wealth or intelligence would participate with the common people who are supposed to compose the Democratic party. Unfortunately for Mr. Bookwalter, in 1880 death took from his side his best friend and counselor, his wife. His life and home were left disconsolate. He was a changed man. He had a sorrow and a bad liver. His friends, to divert his mind, flattered him with the pospects of political honors. The mention of his name for Governor pleased him. He had more money than he knew what to do with. He was honorable, conscientious and sensitive. He was willing to be assessed and spend his money legitimately for political honors. Those whom he trusted took advantage of this fact, and placed his money "where it would do the most good." When a rich man turns his attention to politics for the purpose of amusing himself, he and his money become dangerous forces in the body politic. As soon as Mr. Bookwalter's managers opened his "bar'l," the Democrats for "revenue only" began gathering around it and him with uncovered heads and reverential manner. Agents were sent out over the state to sing his praises and persuade the court-house politicians that Mr. Bookwalter "was the man." Money was liberally supplied to make the canvass for Bookwalter delegates at the primaries and conventions. The Columbus *Times*, the central organ of the Democracy, was owned and edited by John H. Putnam and John G. Thompson. It was in favor of John F. Follet for Governor. It was suddenly converted and declared in favor of Mr. Bookwalter.

It was charged that this paper changed candidates for a price in hand paid, and two years later Mr. John F. Follett, as a member of Congress, helped to defeat John G. Thompson for Sergeant-at-Arms of the National House of Representatives, for his unaccountable treachery in this campaign. Mr. Putnam, as a friend of Mr. Pendleton, was sent to the Sandwich Islands by President Cleveland, during his first term. The people and politicians are forgetful and forgiving.

IV. The mysterious strength being developed by Mr. Bookwalter, alarmed many of the "Mossbacks." His managers had availed themselves of the Payne organization of the year before, and as the Standard Oil Combination had no political deviltry on hand in Ohio, these potent agents in Ohio politics were granted leave of absence, with the understanding that they would come when they were called. Raising his hand and holding up two fingers, Mr. Dave Paige said: "In two years we will take the machinery and run it," nodding his head toward the men in the State House, where the State Central Committee was in session organizing and electing an Executive Committee. This was at the Bookwalter convention in 1881.

For the purpose of holding off the Bookwalter movement an attempt was made to induce Allen G. Thurman to be a candidate. He was in Europe, and in June a letter was received from him, written in Paris, declining to permit the use of his name. This removed the only apparent obstacle in Mr. Bookwalter's path to success, and his managers worked with a vigor, stimulated by ample resources. On the 2nd of July, the country was startled by the shooting down of President Garfield. This sad event and the lingering sickness that followed, cast a gloom over the land, and kept the people in an agony of suspense. The Democratic convention met at Columbus a few days after this calamity. The convention was a large one. Mr. Bookwalter's managers had provided free transportation for the workingmen from various places, and they were on hand in large numbers, clamoring for their employer. The indications the night before the convention, pointed to Mr. Bookwalter's nomination, but he was bitterly opposed. It was said that he was a recent convert, and had not been in the party long enough to entitle him to such an honor, as that to which he aspired. It is unfortunate that there had been no rule established fixing the length of time a man must belong to a party before he can aspire to office. Such a provision would be eminently wise, as it would save much feeling and useless argument and wild declamation.

Judge Geddes was also being bitterly opposed by Mr. Barney Burns, S. S. Bloom and others from his own county. He had once been a Whig, but although he had been a Democrat for years before Mr. Bookwalter carried a torch, yet he was not eligible. The same argument was used against Gen. Banning, who became a Democrat since the war. The most effective statement used against Mr. Bookwalter, was by a gentleman from Cincinnati, who said: "The strongest argument being used for Mr. Bookwalter, is that he is a wealthy man and has money to spend. This will only be a declaration to the Republicans that we have nominated a man because he has money, and they have always been able to lay down ten dollars where the Democrats put one into the campaign."

Mr. John H. Thomas had appeared at the convention of the Clarke County Democrats and had endorsed Mr. Bookwalter in glowing language, yet he had written a letter, it was claimed, saying, "that it would be a calamity to the Democratic party to nominate Mr. Bookwalter," and he was on the ground doing quiet and effective work against the candidacy of his fellow townsmen. The politicians raised on the lime-stone soil of the Mad River Valley, have a strong penchant for locking horns with each other. Most of the distinguished gentlemen who were candidates were on the ground engaged in the idiotic task of shaking hands, saying little and looking wise. To Mr. Bookwalter's credit it must be said, that he remained at home and refused to attempt in any personal way to influence the delegates.

A platform on state issues was adopted. Nine candidates were presented to the convention. On the first ballot, Bookwalter got 208½ votes, Follett 123, Geddes 104½, Banning 61, Miller 32, Jewett 23, Thoman 49, Cook 33, and Armstrong 47. On the second ballot Bookwalter received 386½ votes, Follett 192½, Geddes 57, Banning 32, Miller 9, Jewett 6, and Cook 5. In the Hamilton County delegation, the vote was divided on the first ballot as follows: Bookwalter 12, Follett 2, Banning 17, Miller 17, Cook 10. On the second ballot this vote was divided as follows: Bookwalter 26, Follett 20, and Banning 14. Mr. Bookwalter was declared the nominee. The Republican press charged that the nomination had been secured by money. One paper put a cut of a silver dollar over the convention proceedings, and called it "Bookwalter's boom."

The Democratic press retaliated by printing a $ mark as a photograph of Charles Foster. Both were right. Boodle was Boss. Gov. Foster had boodle-ized Ohio, and compelled the Democrats to imitate his methods. Not less than $20,000 of Mr. Bookwalter's money had been spent to secure the nomination, and $40,000 was spent between the convention and the election. This went almost entirely to newspapers for extra circulation, and to committees for organization. The condition of the President and his death made the campaign a gloomy and difficult one. There was no stumping campaign. The "Mossbacks" sulked in their tents, and not a single leader lifted his voice in favor of the ticket. The State Executive Committee was organized against Mr. Bookwalter, with Mr. Clark Irvine at the head of it. Everything was done that he could devise to "bleed" the candidate and help the enemy. Mr. Bookwalter's assessment was fixed at $20,000, and reduced to $6,000. He paid $5,000 and conducted his campaign without the committee. Mr. John G. Thompson and Mr. John H. Putnam, of the Columbus *Times*, went to Springfield with a letter from the Executive Committee, and made a bold demand for $1,000 as the price of the support of their paper. Mr. Bookwalter was astonished. This was the first time he had been asked personally for money. It was a revelation to him. His managers had kept all these ugly things in the background. He indignantly refused to pay a cent. The morning after his defeat the Columbus *Times*, after taking pay to support Mr. Bookwalter for the nomination, and having aided materially in that result, openly repudiated and assailed him. It was a pitiable and shameful performance. Mr. Bookwalter's refusal to recognize the executive committee, completed the demoralization of the campaign. He anticipated his defeat, and said he would be beaten by the "Mossbacks." He was not disappointed. He received 288,426; Foster, 312,735; the Prohibitionists, 16,597; the Greenbackers, 6,330; and scattering, 138. Mr. John Seitz, the author of the law to preserve the "purity of elections," was the Greenback candidate for Governor.

V. The events surrounding Mr. Garfield's death, and the advent of Mr. Arthur in the White House, had disgusted Republicans and demoralized the party. The Prohibition vote had been growing in Ohio, and coming largely from the Republican ranks. The defection was a cause for apprehension. Under the leadership of Gov. Foster an attempt was made to placate this element, and to raise additional revenues by the Pond and Scott laws, to tax saloons. These laws were declared unconstitutional, and while they did not please the Prohibitionists, they excited the opposition of the powerful brewing, liquor and saloon elements. In 1882, the issue raised by the laws mentioned, was the leading one. The Republicans nominated Mr. Chas. Townsend, of Athens, for Secretary of State, and the Democrats chose Mr. James W. Newman, of Portsmouth. There was little money used in the campaign. But little was needed to pay legitimate expenses. There was no Legislature to be chosen, and no great prizes to struggle for, and the "silent and abhorrent forces" remained in abeyance. A total of 635,095 votes were cast, of which the Democrats polled 316,874; the Republicans, 297,795; the Prohibitionists, 16,597; the Greenbackers, 5,345, and 2,915 scattering. The Democrats had carried Ohio by nearly 20,000 plurality, in the fourth largest vote ever cast in the state, in a moneyless campaign.

At this point it is proper to call attention to a remarkable transaction. For the first time in the history of Ohio, an open charge was made that members of the Legislature had been offered bribes, and some that had not been offered money, called attention to their presence on earth by soliciting some of the wealth that Alex. Sands, Jno. D. Watson and Albert Netter, as lobbyists, were distributing. The Legislature elected the fall before, with Gov. Foster, was Republican in both branches. It organized on a Boodle basis, by selecting Hon. O. B. Hodges, of Cleveland, as Speaker. Mr. Hodges had served several terms in the Legislature, and was the boon companion, and bosom friend and useful ally of Alex. Sands. A big fight was being made to gobble a portion of the canals in Cincinnati for railroad purposes. Money and stock were offered to members for their votes and influence. A reporter hid under a bed in a room used by the lobby, and overheard some damaging details. Money was paid to a member. These charges were printed. Speaker Hodges, who in his innocence and purity, had doubted the presence of such a thing as a lobby, even when he sat in a poker game with the agents and was permitted to win, arose in the House, after prayer at the opening by Rev. Thomas Lee, who thoughtfully informed God of some of the temptations that surround Legislatures, and in sorrowful tones informed the members that some of their number had not only been bribed but had been indiscreet enough to be caught. A committee of seven was promptly ordered by the House in response to the touching appeal of its chief officer, and steps were taken to protect the honorable members and the honorable lobby by suppressing the facts. But a heedless and inconsiderate Grand Jury convened in April, and indicted Jno. D. Watson for bribing and offering bribes to members; and indicted two members, Mr. Bloch, of Cleveland, a Republican, and Wm. A. Wright, of Hocking, a Democrat, for accepting and soliciting bribes. Poor Watson had run out of money, and abandoned by friends, he was promptly sent to the penitentiary. The members escaped and were permitted to serve out their terms in the House instead of the penitentiary. It was poetic and appropriate that this harvest should ripen while Mr. Foster was Governor of Ohio. It was the legitimate fruit of a Legislature conceived in rascality and born in corruption.

BOODLE RESERVATION.

(*Porcupine, Dec. 1890.*)

CHAPTER IX.

A FOUNTAIN OF GOLDEN GREASE.—THE HOADLY CAMPAIGN OF 1883.—THE PAYNE PURCHASE.—A CARNIVAL OF CORRUPTION.—THE COMMUNISM OF WEALTH.

HERE I wish to say a word about communism—the communism of wealth. In the last Legislature, when a bill was pending to abolish the infamous convict contract and slave system in the Ohio Penitentiary, Jno. F. Locke, a member of the House from Madison, said: "This measure is in the interests of communism and lawlessness, and the men who are demanding its passage, are no better than red-handed Nihilists and Communists." Our acceptation of the term "communist," is, that it is one who favors laws that will give him an interest in other people's property without giving something of value in return. If this be a correct definition of communism, I have found in eleven years experience in our legislative halls as a reporter, that the most reckless, brazen, desperate communists in our fair, free land, are men of money, who surround our legislators to tempt, bribe and seduce them, to pass laws, not for the welfare of the whole people, but in behalf of corporations and monopoly. This is the communism of wealth. This is the communism that has transformed our government, in one hundred years, from a representative to a misrepresentative form of government. It is the communism of unscrupulous wealth, that has made scandals like flocks of buzzards, hover over our capitals. It is this kind of communism that has led to such deplorable acts in the past few years, that we have become a by-word and a hissing among the nations of the earth. There is more danger to our free institutions from this kind of communism, than from all the strikes that can occur. The daring and dangerous methods of corporate and dishonest wealth constitute a communism that creates all the discontent of honest labor. This is the kind of communism that defiantly says, that the masses and the honest toiler have no rights in our boasted free government, that money is bound to respect.—*Speech of Allen O. Myers, on the east front of the Capitol, Columbus, O., July 14, 1883.*

I. We have reached the climax of the story of "Bosses and Boodle in Ohio Politics." Emerson says "that England reaches to the Alleghanies, but America begins in Ohio." We have boasted with a pardonable pride of Ohio men and their achievements. But the forces and conditions that have produced these results, have afforded opportunities equally as great for unparalleled evil. The father of all trusts was born in Ohio, and grew out of an Ohio corporation. Trusts and tramps were bred by the same parents. The industrial conditions that made trusts possible, made tramps a certainty. These two phenomena are the natural and extreme results of outraged and violated laws of the state and of trade. The Standard

Oil Company is about to glide upon the scene with soft and silent tread. Corporations have no souls. The Standard Oil Company has no politics. It knows no difference between prayer and politics, between preachers and politicians, between creeds and constitutions, and has no respect for any or all of them. It has no God but gain. It fears no Devil but loss.

II. Oil was discovered and utilized in America in 1860. Its production from the earth, refinement and sale created one of the greatest of modern industries. There was a free market for the crude oil and the manufactured and refined oil, and its by-products found ready and profitable sale. There was healthy competition between buyers and sellers, producers and consumers, manufacturers and traders, and living rates for shippers. In 1862, crude oil was worth ten cents a barrel. In ten years from the discovery, 6,000,000 barrels of oil were produced annually, and $200,000,000 of capital and 60,000 people were employed in this great industry. In 1862, a man who had been a clerk, book-keeper and partner in a country produce store in Cleveland, started a small oil refinery in Cleveland. He took as partners, a brother, an English mechanic, and later another partner, who had been a "clerk in a country store," and had been successful, on a small scale, in the salt and lumber business. Later five others were taken into the obscure and unknown firm, on terms of equality. The Standard Oil Company was incorporated under the laws of Ohio, to engage in the manufacture and sale of petroleum oil, for illuminating and "other purposes," but chiefly for "other purposes." The firm started with $10,000 capital, on paper. One of them conceived the idea of controlling the output and the market, and fixing their own prices. To do this it would be necessary to control railroads and freight rates. A combination was formed and a contract was made with the New York Central, Lake Shore, Erie, and Pennsylvania railroad companies, to raise rates and pay a rebate of one-half to the Standard Oil Company, on all oil shipped by it and other companies. This unlawful and rascally combination was known as the South Improvement Company. There were thirteen men in this company, ten of whom were members of the Standard Oil Company, including all of the officers and a majority of the directors of that corporation. The rest were railroad men. In March, 1872, rates east from the oil regions of Pennsylvania were put up from $1.25 to $2.84 a barrel. It is estimated that the first year this increased rate realized $7,500,000, of which $6,000,000 went into the pockets of the oil trust. The business was paralyzed. The selling price of crude oil was seventy cents less per barrel than the cost of production. The panic came in 1873, but the Trust did not suffer. While prices declined in every branch of business, the Cleveland crowd kept up the price of kerosene. They reduced production and raised profits from 34 cents to $2.05 per barrel, and cleared $315,000 on a $10,000 investment in four years.

In 1877, $3,000,000 was cleared on a capital of $3,000,000, and in five years the undivided profits increased the capital to $70,000,000. Mark the astounding progress. Oil discovered in 1860. Refinery started in 1862, on $10,000. Began to shut out competition in 1865. Capital had grown in 1870 to $1,000,000. The combination formed with railroads, to kill competition and destroy business rivals, in 1872, capital $2,500,000. In 1875, capital $3,500,000; in 1882, capital $70,000,000; in 1887, capital $90,000,000; in 1888, capital $148,000,000, and in 1892, capital $166,500,000; and in 1889, the private income of the founder of the first trust was $20,000,000, or three times the amounts paid in dividends by the Bank of England after an existence of two hundred years.

The earth belongs to the Standard Oil Company and the fullness thereof. They own railroads, pipe lines, refineries, steamships, gas wells, oil wells, coal mines, rolling mills, manufactories, legislatures, governors, judges, Congress, councils, cities and states, and also the press. They dictate laws, they write judicial decisions, they elect Senators, they appoint cabinet officers, they buy Senates, they nominate Presidents, they defeat investigations, they defy Congress, they dictate treaties with foreign nations, they make tariff laws, they play with legislators, and in the language of Vanderbilt, they say, "the public be damned." The people for the time being are helpless, but not without hope.

During the gold excitement in 1848-50, when thousands pushed westward over the plains for California, the trail was marked by the skeletons of animals, the graves of those who perished and the abandoned wagons and the refuse of camps. What appalling wrecks are strewn along the triumphant pathway of the Standard Oil Company, in its march to its land of millions! Idle derricks, deserted plants, smokeless refineries, ruined towns, mortgaged homes, rivals driven out of business, competition killed, prices raised, freight rates increased, workingmen idle, families starving, endless litigation, injunctions, investigations, perjuries committed, crimes inspired, deeds of violence, arson incited, murders attempted, widows and women robbed, orphans defrauded, law trampled under foot, courts laughed at, authority spit upon, government defied, and a people enslaved. Oh, what a spectacle for a free land! Are a free people powerless against this monster? We have religious and political liberty, but we are industrial slaves. We spent over three billions of money, and slaughtered hundreds of thousands of our sons; we smeared the land with gore; we incarnadined our seas, and our rivers ran red with the blood of our children; we piled our dead in heaps on a thousand fields; we widowed the fair and made orphans of the young; we have burdened ourselves and generations yet unborn with debt, that the poor black man might be free and that our government might live; but with the close of that terrible conflict, and by the opportunities it made possible, the unlawful combinations of wealth have enslaved the entire people, and seventy millions pay tribute to the multi-millionaires.

Let us proceed with the recital of one of the ordinary crimes and achievements of the Standard Oil Company.

III. Under the leadership of Gov. Foster, a Republican Legislature had passed the Scott law, to tax saloons and raise a revenue thereby. The Pond law had been declared unconstitutional and the Scott law was drawn to avoid its objectionable features. This continued the agitation and aroused the liquor interest and the liberal element. Two amendments to the constitution, relating to the liquor traffic, were submitted to the people, one in favor of prohibiting the traffic, and the other to place the matter under legislative control. Gov. Foster was ambitious to go to the United States Senate, and was hopeful that the legislature would be Republican. As usual, when he wanted anything he had his agents out over the state working to secure the nomination and election of candidates who favored him. There was only one candidate prominently mentioned for the Republican nomination for Governor, and that was Joseph B. Foraker, a popular young lawyer of Hamilton County. To further his own ambitions, Gov. Foster wanted Senator John Sherman to run for Governor. An attempt was made to nominate him, but Mr. Sherman nipped the effort in the bud.

The Republican State Convention met in Columbus the first week in June. It was a large but not a noisy nor an enthusiastic gathering. Mr. Foraker was nominated by acclamation.

The Democratic State Convention had been called to meet Wednesday, June 20th. There were two prominent candidates in the field seeking the nomination for Governor, Geo. Hoadly of Cincinnati, and Durbin Ward of Lebanon. The son of the Puritan and one of "the people to the South," were revolving in the same orbit, and were again in opposition. Geo. Hoadly was born in New Haven, Conn., July 31, 1825. Durbin Ward was born in Augusta, Ky., Feb. 11, 1819.

Mr. Hoadly came of good English stock. His great-grandmother was a daughter of Jonathan Edwards, and married Timothy Dwight. Mr. Hoadly's father was a graduate of Yale. He failed in business, and in 1830 he removed with his family to Cleveland, O. Here Geo. Hoadly grew up. He went to Western Reserve College, and graduated from Harvard Law School. In 1846, young Hoadly went to Cincinnati and entered the law office of Salmon P. Chase. He had a fine mind, was studious and untiring in his work, and quickly grasped and applied to practice the great principles of his profession. His habits were good, his character excellent, his manner affable, and success early crowned his efforts. At twenty-five he was chosen a judge of the Superior Court of Cincinnati, and in this responsible place he became familiar with the details of commercial law and practice, such as grow up in great commercial centers. This training, with his ready tact and natural gifts, fitted him for his subsequent career as one of the most successful corporation lawyers in Cincinnati, if not in the country. He declined all political preferment, and devoted himself to his growing and lucrative practice, except the few months spent as a member of the constitutional convention. As lawyer, Mr. Hoadly stood at the head of his profession, as a citizen he was honored and respected. With a noble wife his home and family were happy, and he had little that the rational mind or the heart of man could desire. But his tireless and active brain was as restless as a caged bird. He was in the thick of every intellectual fray, on every important question that was before the public. The only place he blundered was in politics, and at this he was a master. His is one of the most grotesque figures that has ever played across the great stage of Ohio politics. He was a Democrat, when he fell under the shadow of Chase's great influence. He joined the Anti-Slavery Democrats, became a Free Soiler, was a Union man, became a Republican, joined the Liberals 1872, and then joined the Democrats again. It is but just to Mr. Hoadly to say that he never changed his politics. It was the parties that changed and left him, only to return. In 1876 he tried to make the electoral commission believe that one of Mr. Tilden's electors had been chosen in Oregon. He convinced "7" of the commission but "8" refused to agree with him, and he had lost his case and Mr. Tilden the Presidency. The latter, however, was grateful to Mr. Hoadly, and was willing to promote his political ambitions. Mr. Hoadly appeared as a Tilden-Payne delegate in the Cincinnati convention in 1880, and his conduct was unworthy his past career, and brought discredit on his good name. It is hard to understand why men, whose acts have been above reproach in all the other walks of life, seem willing to resort to any baseness, the moment they venture into the fields of politics. Ambition! Ambition! Must be the transforming power that converts an upright man into a devil of evil purposes and wicked determination.

Geo. Hoadly had worked hard all his life-time. He wanted a rest, but his active mind could not brook idleness. He sought a change of occupations. He wanted a congenial field that would give wider scope to his splendid gifts. He wanted to be President of the United States. He thought the Governorship of Ohio would be a stepping-stone. He wanted to be Governor of Ohio. He did not wait for the honor to seek him. He sought it.

IV. An effort is being made to erect a statue in honor of Durbin Ward. If the men who took money and those who gave it, when Durbin Ward was alive, to prevent him from becoming Governor of Ohio, will contribute as liberally to the fund, the monument will soon be completed, and stand as a deserving honor to a man who was faithful to his convictions, in a day and generation that betrayed him for base bribes. Mr. Ward's parents were of English and Welsh extraction, and came to Kentucky from Maryland. The family was poor. When a child, his parents removed to Fountain County, Indiana. Here young Ward worked on a farm and got all the knowledge he could acquire in the "log school house on Poplar Ridge." The boy loved books, and eagerly read all that he could procure. At nineteen he went to Miami University, at Oxford, O. Among his fellow students was Geo. E. Pugh. Mr. Ward taught school to secure the money necessary to pay his way at college. He left college after two years study, located at Lebanon, O., and began the study of law. He was admitted to the bar in 1843, and became a partner of Thomas Corwin. He was elected prosecuting attorney of Warren County, and served six years. In 1851 he was chosen a member of the Ohio Legislature as a Whig. He opposed the Knownothings, and when the Republican party was formed, he became a Democrat, and in 1856 was a candidate for Congress on that ticket. In 1857 he was the Democratic candidate for

Attorney General and was defeated. He was opposed to slavery and was an ardent supporter of Stephen A. Douglas. When the war broke out he enlisted as a private in Company F, 12th Ohio Volunteers. He served with honor and was rapidly promoted, and at the close of the war, he had earned a Brigadier General's commission. In 1863 he was the major of the 17th Ohio Infantry, and while it was stationed at Triune, Tenn., in April, he wrote a letter to Thomas Milliken, to be read at a Union meeting held in Hamilton, O., in response to an invitation to be present and speak. He said: "We are in the face of the enemy and I cannot quit the field for any purpose." He was opposed to Vallandingham and favored Democratic equality, the Constitution and the Union. It was in this letter that Durbin Ward used the famous phrase, "*I am a Democrat*," which has since been used by others, when it did not require any courage to make the announcement. In 1866 he ran against Gen. Robt. S. Schenck for Congress and was beaten, and was appointed United States District Attorney by President Johnson. In 1877 he was defeated by R. M. Bishop for the nomination for Governor. Durbin Ward was not pliant enough either as man, politician or lawyer, for the shifting age in which he lived. As a politician he refused to abandon his convictions of a lifetime for an evasive party policy; as a lawyer he believed in the principles of his profession. He would not play with phrases. He did not believe the law capable of two constructions, and he could not be tempted by a fee to change sides, or to construe a law against its plain intent and purpose. He was not a rich man. He did not believe in corrupting the people. He was opposed to the use of money in politics. For these reasons he was a failure as a politician, and he never was and never could be a successful corporation lawyer. The Constitution was his bible of law and the creed of his politics. He died May 22, 1886. There was a great demonstration at his funeral. He was more popular dead than alive. Such men always are. In an eulogy delivered by Mr. Geo. W. Houk of Dayton, he said of Durbin Ward: "There was not an hour or an occasion in his life when he would not have chosen defeat, rather than to have achieved success by a dishonorable, unfaithful or corrupt act.

V. In 1881 David R. Paige held up two fingers and said, "two years from now we want this organization." The time of which David spoke was at hand. He was chairman of the Democratic State Central Committee, and had been elected a member of Congress in part recognition of the useful services he had rendered the Payne branch of the Standard Oil Company.

Perhaps there had never been a contest in Ohio, in which there were so many cross purposes, and so many conflicting interests, as this one we are describing. Geo. H. Pendleton's term in the Senate was about to expire, and the Legislature to be elected would choose his successor. He was a candidate for re-election. He and Mr. Hoadly being citizens of Cincinnati, their interests would conflict, as it was not politic to take the Senator and Governor of a great state from one locality. They met, and Mr. Hoadly frankly told Mr. Pendleton his ambitions. The latter, as ever, was amiable and complaisant, and agreed not to interfere with the aspirations of the other. Washington McLean and Mr. Pendleton had quarreled over some personal matter, and there was a bitter feud between them, and the enmity spread to their friends and families. It manifested itself in social life, in politics and in business. John R. McLean took up his father's fight against Pendleton. The Scotch blood of the McLeans made itself manifest, in the propensity to transmit the family feuds with the family name and property, from sire to son. John R. McLean is one of the most remarkable and enigmatical men Ohio has ever produced. His father was a prosperous boiler manufacturer in Cincinnati when the son was born. He became interested in politics and purchased an interest in the Cincinnati *Enquirer*. The son attended the schools in Cincinnati, and for a brief season was a student at Yale. He was bright, quick and full of animal life. He had no passion for books. He loved outdoor sports, and preferred a game of base ball, or a glove contest to poetry, prose or problems. He had one ever-ruling passion as a boy. It was in accord with the spirit of the age. He wanted to be rich. He wanted to be rich quick. Mr. McLean is not a miser. He does not love money for itself. He worships it for the power it brings. With it he believes anything is possible, without it he doubts if anything can be achieved. He has no morals. He is a stranger to sentiment. He is not deterred by scruples. If he has an object in view, and has the money to buy it, and wants to buy it, in his code of life, no law, no man, no community has a right to question his act. He believes every man has his price. He goes straight to results, and cares nothing about public opinion, methods or the rights of others. When he can get or has got what he wants, he pays for it promptly and liberally.

It don't seem possible that such a character can exist in an enlightened age. But John R. McLean is a fact, whose existence must be acknowledged. It may be studied but not denied. It is said that he got his first money by backing a blind printer, Sine, in a lottery venture. At twenty-five, by purchase and gift from his father and uncle, he had acquired a majority of the stock and control of the *Cincinnati Enquirer*. He did not know much about the newspaper business, but he had an instinctive knowledge of the force and value of men, and he quickly gathered a staff of bright writers and able men upon his paper. He watched its finances and guided its destinies at all times himself. The paper prospered. Everything he touched turned to gold. At thirty he had realized the dream of his boyhood. He was a millionaire. But he was suffering with the new disease. He had the "passion for accumulation." He wanted "more," he said, and he could not get enough. They never do. They never can. With his money and his newspaper, Mr. John R. McLean had become one of the most potent factors in the business and political affairs of Ohio.

VI. There were many Democrats who revolted at Mr. McLean's methods as an editor and a Democrat. In this they did him an injustice. Mr. McLean never had any political convictions. The passing views he may have had from day to day, he discarded when he changed his shirt. He never had any convictions upon *any* question. He had neither time nor disposition to be troubled with them. He could not use them in his business, but could use and amuse himself with the party. As an organization it was an instrument in his hands to punish his own and his father's enemies. He had no friends to reward. He hired his men, and when the money was paid the contract was closed. But there were a great many men who both hated and feared Mr. McLean and his newspaper. As a counter-irritant a number of them are said to have put up their money to start the *News-Journal.* This enterprise met with Mr. McLean's hearty disapproval. Mr. Hoadly and Mr. Pendleton were among the supporters of the new paper. This drove Mr. McLean to do the most commendable act of his life. He supported Durbin Ward for Governor. His support was as surprising as it was fatal, as his intentions were distrusted, but he spent his money lavishly. Geo. Hoadly called to his aid such agents as Alex. Sands, and they visited the counties, and a conflict took place at every county seat over the election of delegates. It was a desperate hand to hand struggle. Every inch of ground was contested, and not a delegate was overlooked. More money was spent in the preliminary contest in fighting each other, than the Democrats had ever spent in a campaign against the Republicans. Mr. Pendleton had his agents out working to secure the nomination of men for the Legislature who were favorable to his re-election to the Senate. The "silent and abhorrent forces" of the Standard Oil Company, were listless and apparently took no part. Oliver Payne said in his club at Cleveland, that he preferred Ward to Hoadly, but this was for public effect. It would never do to let the Democrats or the people know that the Standard Oil Company had a candidate for Governor and one for Senator. If it became public it meant the certain defeat of both. Mr. Hoadly's candidacy was a logical one to some extent, as he was the leading attorney for the liquor and brewing interests in the suit to test the constitutionality of the Scott law. As the time for the convention approached, the contest grew fierce and furious. The forces were evenly divided. In Hamilton, Butler County, where Durbin Ward had always been an idol and very popular, as it was in his Senatorial and Congressional district, Mr. Hoadly's money was used, and delegates were selected and instructed for Mr. Hoadly.

This raised such a just storm of indignation, that the "Bosses" did not dare to carry it out. There was a battle royal in Hamilton County for the 68 votes. Of these Mr. McLean succeeded in electing 26 for Durbin Ward, leaving 42 for Mr. Hoadly, but before Mr. McLean could deliver his goods, 13 of them and a fraction of one vote got away from him, and he only had 12½ left. The convention met Thursday, June 21st.

Mr. John McSweeney was selected by the Payne managers as chairman. This did not arouse suspicion, as Mr. McSweeney stood well with the Thurman people. Mr. McSweeney had a Payne heart, with a Thurman outside. He was utterly unfitted for the difficult duties of chairman, but he proved very useful in doing the particular work at an important crisis, for which he was chosen. In its description of the convention, the *Cincinnati Enquirer*, of June 22, 1883, says: "The Democratic State Convention of to-day, was probably the noisiest, the most disorderly and altogether the most remarkable political gathering Columbus has ever seen. It exhibited a great deal of earnestness, eloquence and aggressiveness, but was also notable for monumental foolishness and *a few instances that led to accusations of crookedness!*"

Mr. Pendleton had directed his energies and influence toward gaining control of the Committee on Resolutions, and the result was a ringing and emphatic rehearsal of all that the Democrats of Ohio had said in previous platforms on civil service, and an unequivocal endorsement of the same. The convention swallowed it without a question. The Standard Oil Company shut their eyes. They could not afford to unmask their designs at this time, and Mr. Pendleton was splendidly vindicated, and although not named in the resolutions, he and his many ardent friends felt that he was the logical and only candidate for Senator. But alas, there were others! Judge Hoadly and the other candidates for Governor were on the ground.

The strain on the nervous temperament of Mr. Hoadly was something terrible. His whole nature, teachings and life, had been opposed to the methods that were being employed to secure his nomination. Cato says, "that corruption never lacks a pretense," and Mr. Hoadly justified his conduct, on the ground that dishonest means and bribery were being used by Jno. R. McLean and others to defeat and humiliate him. "Archbishop" Sands, the great comforter, was ever near to explain and soothe the poor man's conscience. Mr. Hoadly was desperate. He said, just before the convention met, that he would have the nomination, if it cost him $20,000. As high as $250 was paid a number of the 56 delegates from Hamilton County who voted for Mr. Hoadly. Some of them had previously taken Mr. McLean's money; several of them sold so often, that they forgot which side had bought them last.

The convention, when it met, lost no time in getting down to business. The "Bosses and the Boodlers" were there and eager for the market to open, with eloquent John McSweeney as chief auctioneer. Durbin Ward's name was presented by Hon. T. E. Powell, and seconded by Allen G. Thurman, who made a strong, touching and eloquent plea for honest Durbin. Mr. Michael Ryan, of Cincinnati, presented Mr. Hoadly's name, and Gen. G. W. Morgan nominated Hon. Geo. W. Geddes. The balloting began amidst great excitement and a tremendous uproar. When Butler County was reached, an attempt was made to cast her 13 votes for Hoadly. Objection was made, and a storm broke loose, such as was rarely ever seen in a convention. The chairman seemed dazed and powerless. He hammered on a table with a heavy cane, which only added to the tempest. A Ward man moved that each delegate cast his vote as he saw fit. Judge Spalding, of Cleveland, moved to lay this motion on the table. This motion was put and the roll call ordered. On the motion to lay on the table, there were 312 ayes and 323 noes. This was a test vote, and showed Hoadly in a minority and beaten. The chair neglected or refused to put the motion to allow each delegate to cast his vote, but this was done and the ballot for Governor proceeded. The chair announced that Hoadly had received 290 votes, Ward 261½, Geddes 77, and Denver 4½ on the first ballot. It required 318 votes to nominate. There was no nomination; a second ballot was proceeded with, amidst unparalleled confusion. The Ward delegates openly charged fraud at the secretary's table. They tried to get on the stage, but the Hoadly men surrounded the secretaries and prevented all approach. There were few changes, and no stampeding. The forces stood firm. The Geddes men tried to change to Ward, but the Hoadly men yelled so that no one could be heard. The secretaries were nearly an hour in making the footings. Everybody tried to get on the stage, and as its capacity was limited, many failed, but fell off trying. The chair finally got the sheets and announced the vote as follows: Hoadly 332, Ward 245, scattering 60, and he declared Hoadly the nominee. This was greeted with cries of "fraud," and "you are a liar." The ballot as shown by counties, as it has been preserved, was: Ward 270, Hoadly 315, and 50 for Geddes. Judge Hoadly had not been nominated, but in the "interest of harmony," Mr. Powell moved to make the nomination unanimous, amidst cries of "no! no! don't encourage fraud!" The conflict had lasted five hours. John R. McLean was named on a committee to escort Judge Hoadly to the hall. He appeared, and "with a heart overflowing with emotion," thanked the convention for having preferred a "recruit" to the faithful of the fold. All feeling seemed to vanish and in one of those many and unaccountable moods that often overtake great bodies of men, they sent for Gen. Durbin Ward. His speech was full of lament and pathos. It brought tears to many eyes and awakened sorrow in many hearts. He closed by saying that he would be a candidate for United States Senator, but he said: "*I shall not use one dollar to procure my election to the United States Senate.*" He was greeted with cheers at the close of one of the most remarkable speeches ever made to a political convention. But we are living in an age full of transformation scenes, and the Standard Oil Company had purchased its first state convention. Judge Hoadly is credited with saying, that his nomination had cost $50,000. Again the sons of the Puritan and the children of New England had combined with corruption and vanquished one of "the people to the South."

VII. The results of this convention dazed John R. McLean. "Jack had found his master." Mr. McLean had found forces more potent than his own methods, and a pocket-book greater than his purse. It set him to thinking. He wanted to beat Mr. Pendleton. He must divide and conquer. He and Mr. Hoadly made an alliance. The *Enquirer* was to give Mr. Hoadly a cordial support for Governor, and he was to sever all connection with the *News-Journal* and cut off its supplies. The bargain was kept; the *News-Journal* soon died. Mr. Pendleton was left alone to face Mr. McLean. The celebrated Highland House Convention was held in Cincinnati, August 18th. It is said to have cost Mr. McLean $20,000. He named every man on the ticket. Mr. Pendleton's friends held another convention and nominated another ticket. This was indiscreet, and lost Mr. Pendleton many friends and destroyed his party standing.

With all of these fights, divisions and party scandals it did not seem possible that the Democrats could win, but no party organization ever had such vitality. Mr. Foraker and Mr. Hoadly met in joint debate in a number of the large cities of the state and discussed the liquor question. The liquor and brewing interests contributed freely to the Democratic campaign fund. Mr. Pendleton sent sums ranging from $200 to $1,000 into a number of counties to help elect the Democratic ticket. This money was generally sent to the candidates for the Legislature to place them under personal obligations. The agents of the Standard Oil Company did not take an active part in any of the county nominations, conventions and primaries. They remained quiet until the campaign was well under way. The candidates were "seen," "felt" and "helped." Whenever it was found that Mr. Pendleton had sent any money to a candidate, the Standard Oil Company's agents doubled the amount. The profusion with which money poured in upon many candidates for the Legislature in rural counties overwhelmed and amazed the innocent aspirant for legislative honors. In many instances they were not backward in asking for money from Mr. Pendleton, and when they received it and found that they could get more from the Standard Oil Company's agents they took it. In one or two cases Mr. Pendleton's money was returned, so conscientious were the parties, but these instances were very rare. When the election came Mr. Pendleton had helped candidates in over fifty counties, and held pledges from forty or more to support him if they were elected. There was not a candidate for the Legislature on the Democratic ticket, outside of the large cities, that was not sounded for Mr. Payne, and if found all right he was liberally aided, and to make it appear proper, additional aid was sent through Mr. G. H. Bargar, the chairman of the campaign committee. He sent a letter saying the money was from Mr. Payne's friends, and was to be used to get out the Democratic vote, but there was no allusion to the fact that Henry B. Payne was or would be a candidate for the Senate. This was known to only a few within the inner circle.

Mr. Hoadly broke down during the campaign and withdrew from the canvass, and went to Philadelphia for rest and treatment. It was said that he was suffering from an attack of malaria. He was suffering from the tortures of conscience. Remorse over the acts he had encouraged and countenanced was what caused Geo. Hoadly to break down, and he never recovered and he never will recover from the effects of his wicked conduct in defrauding Durbin Ward of an honor that was justly his. The sickness of their candidate discouraged the Democrats, but did not demoralize them. Boodle flowed in golden streams from the fountain placed on tap by the Standard Oil Company. The election was held in October, and the Democrats elected their entire state ticket and carried the Legislature by a safe majority in both branches. The vote was the largest ever cast at a state election, the total being 721,310, of which Mr. Hoadly received 359,693; Mr. Foraker, 347,164; the Prohibitionists, 8,362; the Greenbackers, 2,937, and scattering, 3,154. Mr. McLean had succeeded in electing his entire ticket in Hamilton County by the lavish use of money, and with the aid of the people.

VIII. After the election was over rumors began to float about that Mr. Payne was or would be a candidate for Senator. Mr. Jno. R. McLean was quite delighted with his venture in politics and his first victory. He had not really determined whether to be a candidate himself or to support his father for the honor, but the signs soon began to convince him that the same mysterious force and silent power, that he had encountered at the state convention in June, was again abroad in the land. His first object was to beat Mr. Pendleton; his next was to name his successor. If he entered into a conflict with the people to the north he would be beaten, be shorn of his prestige, and lose all money he had expended. Mr. McLean never regretted money he spent to buy revenge, but his business sense and his "passion for accumulation" always taught him to keep his eye on the dollar. If he could defeat Mr. Pendleton, and recover his much loved dollars, his cup would be full and running over. He and Oliver Payne met at night in a sleeping car in the central part of the state, and divided the empire.

Mr. McLean claimed to have expended $100,000 in helping carry Hamilton County and elect a Legislature. He was to be reimbursed for all money expended, and was to support Mr. Henry B. Payne for United States Senator, and when he was older he was to have an open field for the honor. A careful comparison of notes was made and the labor divided and men selected, so that there might be no conflict and no confusion. It was very important not to arouse the suspicions of Mr. Pendleton, nor the cupidity of those who were to be purchased, or who had been bought. The delegation from Hamilton County was pledged to Mr. Payne by Mr. McLean as a guarantee of good faith. It was not sold. It was given away.

IX. The Democrats had elected 60 members of the House and 22 Senators, and the Republicans had 44 members of the House and 11 Senators. The members of the Legislature were as follows, the names of the Democrats being in italics.

SENATORS.

1st District, *William Caldwell, W. L. O'Brien, A. J. Pruden;* 2d District, *George F. Elliott;* 3d District, *Simon Brenner;* 4th District *John E. Myers;* 5th District, Jesse N. Oren; 6th District, *William H. Reed;* 7th District, John W. Gregg; 8th District, John H. Evans; 9th District, *Calvin S. Welch;* 10th District, *Aaron R. Van Cleaf;* 11th District, Sylvester W. Durflinger; 12th District, *A. C. Cable;* 13th District, John J. Hane; 14th District, *Gilbert Smith;* 15th and 16th District, *John O'Neill;* 17th and 28 District, *Allen Levering;* 18th and 19th District, *William S. Crowell;* 20th District, Solomon Hogue; 21st District, *John V. Lewis;* 22d District, John M. Dickinson; 23rd District, Alonzo D. Fassett; 24th and 26th District, Simon P. Wolcott; 25th District, *A. J. Williams;* George H. Ely; 27th and 29th District, Timothy G. Loomis; 30th District, *Godfrey Jaeger;* 31st District, *John H. Williston;* 32d District, *Thomas J. Godfrey, Elmer White;* 33d District, *William H. McLyman, Orlando B. Ramey.*

MEMBERS OF THE HOUSE OF REPRESENTATIVES.

Charles E. Addison, Muskingum; *David Baker*, Darke: *Gilbert H. Bargar*, Coshocton; David M. Barrett, Highland; *William Beatty*, Lucas; *James T. Black*, Madison; *Henry Bohl*, Washington; Emerson P. Brooks, Meigs; S. W. Brown, Warren; *J. E. Bruce*, Hamilton; *Lewis A. Brunner*, Wyandot; *Robert Buchanan*, Clermont; Charles C. Burnett, Cuyahoga; *Absolom P. Byal*, Hancock; Jesse

L. Cameron, Union; *Thomas J. Cogan*, Hamilton; *L. C. Cole*, Stark; *John Cosgrove*, Hamilton; *Geo. W. Crites*, Tuscarawas; *John Cuff*, Henry; *J. B. Cummings*, Hamilton; *Frank Cunningham*, Butler; Albert Deyo, Fulton; Alexander Dickson, Mahoning; *Oscar F. Edwards*, Montgomery; Elijah P. Emerson, Wood; Wm. M. Farrar, Guernsey; *Wm. W. Fierce*, Vinton; *Levi W. Finley*, Noble; Geo. H. Ford, Geauga and Lake; *J. R. Francisco*, Sandusky; Jos. S. Gaston, Pike; *Henry George*, Defiance and Paulding; Joseph G. Gest, Greene; *Oliver P. Goodman*, Ross; Henry C. Greiner, Perry; *William Habbeler*, Ottawa; Horace L. Hadley, Fayette; *Jas. H. Hamilton*, Monroe; *A. G. Harbaugh*, Cuyahoga; *Robert H. Higgins*, Brown; Samuel Hilles, Belmont; *Geo. W. Holbrook*, Auglaize; Wm. T. Hughes, Van Wert; *George W. Hull*, Allen; *Phannel Hunt*, Shelby; Watson D. Johnson, Huron; *Solomon Johnson*, Williams; Robert H. Jones, Jackson; *Ignatius H. Kahle*, Putnam; Jacob A. Kohler, Summit; Stephen Laird, Trumbull; Jasper N. Lantz, Harrison; Benjamin N. Linduff, Jefferson; *Joseph Lisle*, Licking; John H. Littler, Clarke; *Casper Lowenstein*, Franklin; George W. Love, Columbiana; Cornelius H. Lyman, Medina; *Edward Malone*, Lucas; *A. D. Marsh*, Mercer; Wm. S. Matthews, Gallia; *John McBride*, Stark; *J. B. Menke*, Hamilton; Enos W. Miles, Morrow; *James Mooney*, Cuyahoga; David M. Murray, Miami; *Allen O. Myers*, Franklin; John W. Ogden, Champaign; Wm. Peet, Hamilton; *Joseph M. Poe*, Cuyahoga; Isaac C. Primrose, Athens; *Joseph Puckrin*, Erie; Alfred K. Rarey, Hardin; *Wm. Roche*, Cuyahoga; Enoch C. Ross, Carroll; Daniel J. Ryan, Scioto; George L. Sackett, Delaware; *Wm. A. Schultz*, Fairfield; *George W. Sharp*,

Holmes; Oscar Sheppard, Preble; Aaron M. Sherman, Portage; *David J. Stalter*, Seneca; Elias M. Stanberry, Morgan; *John B. Staubach*, Hamilton; *Andrew Stevenson*, Richland; *Byron Stilwell*, Ashland; *Christopher C. Stouffer*, Wayne; Peter Striker, Hamilton; James H. Terrell, Clinton; *J. R. Thompson*, Hamilton; *John D. Thompson*, Knox; Freeman Thorp, Ashtabula; *James Turner*, Montgomery; James W. Walker, Logan; George G. Washburn, Lorain; *Seth Weldy*, Hocking; Dewitt C. Wilson, Lawrence; *Wesley Work*, Pickaway; *Daniel Wolf*, Hamilton; *John B. Young*, Adams; *Edward W. Young*, Franklin; *Boston G. Young*, Marion; *George M. Ziegler*, Crawford.

Late in October, the Democratic members elect were not content with being visited, but they began to visit; many of them felt called upon to go to Cleveland to look at the building in which the offices of the Standard Oil Company were located, and to find out whom their constituents favored for Senator. They could not find out at home. Newspapers that had been fearless and free in their advocacy of honest Durbin Ward, or courtly George Pendleton, for the Senate, were suddenly taken with the cramp colic, and when they recovered, the next issue, with double leaded vehemence, declared that Henry B. Payne was the only Democrat in Ohio fit to be chosen to the United States Senate. To the honor of the Democratic press of Ohio be it said, that while all were tempted, but few yielded. The sudden conversions always took place after Hon. David R. Paige, on a commercial tour, had dropped "into town to sell some powder." David sold more "powder" in Ohio in a few weeks, than was ever sold before. It was all Standard Oil brand.

The conversion of the press paved the way for the approach of members. Those who had been honest and earnest in their advocacy of Ward or Pendleton, suddenly became silent and indifferent. They had become partners in one of the Standard Oil Company's "adventures," and were receiving their "rebates." The argument used against Mr. Pendleton, was that he was the author of the civil service law. But the platform upon which the state ticket had been elected, and the legislature had been carried, was the most emphatic endorsement of civil service reform, that the Democratic party of Ohio had ever made. The pretext for opposing Mr. Pendleton was the most flimsy and pitiable that could be presented. This feature of the Senatorial canvass only demonstrates the insincerity of political parties and promises.

X. The Legislature convened on the first Monday in January, 1884. The members began to assemble the latter part of New Year's week. All the Senatorial candidates and managers, "Bosses and Boodlers," were early on the ground, except Mr. Henry B. Payne. He did not appear upon the scene until after the purchase had been perfected, and Gov. Hoadly had signed the deed for the property that had been conveyed for a consideration to Mr. Payne, in trust for the Standard Oil Company. Mr. Pendleton's campaign was conducted by Clark Irvin of Knox, Judge J. S. McKemy of Hamilton, John G. Thompson and Geo. B. Okey of Franklin. Durbin Ward's interests were looked after by A. R. Van Cleaf of Pickaway, Wm. Reed of Ross, L. A. Russell of Cleveland, Geo. W. Houk of Dayton, James S. Gordon of Cincinnati, who were honest in their support, and by Geo. Elliott of Butler and others, who betrayed him for a price. The Standard Oil campaign was conducted by Oliver H. Payne, Wm. P. Thompson, John Huntington, David R. Paige, John H. Farley, Martin A. Foran, Elmer White and many other small politicians who were under pay. John R. McLean and his staff, were on hand to watch emergencies. Hundreds of people were furnished transportation and expenses, and were paid to come from all sections of the state, to work for their favorites, but the Payne forces outnumbered the others ten to one.

Preliminary caucuses of the two houses were held by the Democrats on Saturday, January 5, to nominate candidates for officers. A joint caucus was held after the others, and Elmer White, an editor, of Defiance, one of Mr. Payne's supporters, was chosen chairman, L. A. Brunner, another editor and Payne missionary, was made secretary. It was agreed to hold the Senatorial caucus Tuesday night, January 8, a historic day in the annals of the country, and one sacred to the memory and achievements of the greatest apostle of Democracy, St. Jackson. It was a day upon which the Democrats of Ohio had met in convention for many years to declare their principles, nominate their ticket and renew their faith at the altars of Democracy. It was a day which had been looked forward to and honored for years, by gatherings of the gifted sons of genius and of Democracy, when in language that made the heart quicken its pulsations, and in phrases of winning eloquence, the purpose and principles of the organization were declared, and the virtues of its founders were recited, as examples worthy of emulation. It was fitting and particularly appropriate that this day, above all others, should be chosen for the consummation of an act of infamy that would give the lie to every principle that the Democracy had ever professed faith in; heap humiliation on its honored leaders; repudiate its professions, and write shame across the brow of an honored name and a glorious past.

The Payne managers were anxious to hold the caucus as soon as possible, for the wolves had tasted blood, and were growing ravenous with the fleeting hours, and complications might arise that would lead to an explosion. Like the Sanhedrim that sat at midnight and sent Christ to Calvary, "they feared the people." The date was fixed early by the request of Mr. Oliver Payne and John R. McLean, but the choice of the 8th of January, was a piece of irony that they did not appreciate at the time.

A committee of six was appointed to prepare rules for the government of the Senatorial caucus. These were: Senators W. H. McLyman of Toledo, A. R. Van Cleaf of Pickaway, and W. S. Crowell of Coshocton; and the members from the House were: G. H. Bargar of Coshocton, Thos. Cogan of Cincinnati, and Allen O. Myers of Columbus. There was a demand among Democrats that there should be an open vote. The people naturally wanted to know how their honored and chosen representatives voted. The committee to prepare rules met, but could not agree. Mr. Cogan would not attend the meeting. He was doing business upon his own hook and did not want to be considered as one of Mr. McLean's chattels. The committee stood 3 to 2. Messrs. McLyman, Crowell and Bargar very shrewdly framed a report, leaving the caucus to determine whether there should be a secret ballot. The other two favored an open ballot and so reported.

XI. Fixing the date of the caucus at such an early day was an unusual thing, and was evidence to an ordinary mind, that knew anything about politics, that the "Bosses" had purchased votes enough and were eager to proceed. Durbin Ward had telegraphed to L. A. Russell, at Cleveland, on Saturday, to come down and help him. Mr. Russell arrived at midnight, Sunday. Durbin Ward had gone to bed and was asleep. Mr. Russell waked him up and said: "You old pauper, what are you fooling around here for? Don't you know that this thing is bought and paid for, and only waiting for delivery!" Mr. Russell's experience, and his knowledge of the situation, and the men and methods employed by the Standard Oil Company, enabled him to state the case tersely and accurately. Durbin Ward was a doubting Thomas. He said: "Oh, Russell, that can't be so, I will never believe it until I see it done." He saw it done. The canvass continued Monday and Tuesday; never had such a crowd gathered at the capital. The situation was feverish. Bills of large denominations were plenty. Whiskey flowed freely. All was uproar and confusion. Charges of bribery were freely made and faintly denied. Prices ranged from $1200 to $8000 per member. It is but just to say that there were some honest and reputable men in favor of Mr. Payne; but as a rule, every Democrat that had ever been offered or accepted a bribe in politics was there. and was loud in his advocacy of Mr. Payne's election to the Senatorship. The carrion had brought the vultures. David R. Paige's room, on an upper floor, was the paymaster's department. Money was stacked up in piles, to pay members as they were brought in. They got it so easy that some of them came back. It became a matter of common report and belief on Tuesday, that large sums of money were being paid out, and Allen G. Thurman issued the following statement, in the afternoon before the caucus:

"I have nothing against either of the candidates. They are all men of ability. My personal relations with each of them have always been friendly and pleasant. But there is something that shocks me in the idea of crushing men like Pendleton and Ward, who have devoted the best portions of their lives to the maintenance of Democracy, by the combination against them of personal hatred and overgrown wealth. I hear Payne men say: 'We can not support Pendleton because we disapprove of his civil service reform bill,' forgetting that convention after convention of the Democratic party, both State and National, had resolved in favor of civil service reform, and also forgetting that the Republicans now in office are just as liable to be turned out as if the Pendleton bill had never passed. I do not advocate that bill. I think it ought to be amended or repealed; but I would not slaughter a life-long Democrat because in a long public service he happened to make one mistake.

"But if these gentlemen can not support Pendleton, why can not they support Ward? He is not responsible for the civil service reform bill. Indeed, I have always understood that he disapproves of it. That he is a man of ability, every man must admit; that he has performed immense labor for our party, no one will deny. Why, then, prefer Payne to him? The answer, I fear, is perfectly plain. There never has been any machine politics in the Democratic party of Ohio. We have, as a party, been freer from bossism than any party that ever existed. But some men seem to think that we ought to have a machine, amply supplied with money to work it, and under absolute control of a boss or bosses, to dictate who shall and who shall not receive the honors and rewards within the gift of the party. To set up such a machine it is necessary, in the first place, to kill the men who have heretofore enjoyed the confidence of the party—the men whose ability, hard labor, and principles did so much to keep the party together in the terrible ordeal through which it has passed. I am unwilling to see this done. It does not concern me personally, for I am a mere private citizen, having no expectation or wish to ever hold office again. But although I have never sought for revenge upon my enemies in the party—if I have had any—on the other hand, I have never deserted my friends, and I do not want to be called on to be a pall-bearer at their political funerals. I want to see our officers elected in the good old-fashioned Democratic mode, and not by some new-fangled mode that, to say the least of it, wears an evil-omened and inauspicious aspect. I want to see all true Democrats have a fair chance, according to their merits, and do not want to see a political cut-throat bossism inaugurated for the benefit of a close party corporation or syndicate."

The appearance of this chuck of truth, was like the explosion of a bomb. It created great consternation and apprehension among the "Bosses." But the fountain was tapped and the golden grease flowed more freely. Mr. Thurman had only succeeded in bulling the market and raising prices.

The caucus met at 8 P. M., Tuesday, Jan. 8. The Democratic members were all present. Outsiders were all excluded. Great crowds gathered in the adjoining halls and corridors. Members looked at each other with suspicion. Some kept their hands nervously in their pockets. When a man had been paid to vote for Mr. Payne, others who had not been were set to watch him. All the doubtful members had one or two guardians. George Washington Hull of Allen, had been told by Charles Negley of Darke, a well known agent of the Boodlers, that he could get $2,500 for his vote. Mr. Hull swore that when the caucus met, he would arise and state this fact. This would be unpleasant and might make trouble. Mr. A. J. Pruden of Cincinnati, moved that all questions coming before the caucus should be settled without debate. This was indeed a remarkable procedure, but there was so much gun powder lying around loose, that every precaution had to be taken to prevent an explosion. The motion carried and the silent and solemn services of the sale began. The committee on rules made a majority and a minority report. A test vote came first on a slight amendment to the latter. This was to prevent a change of vote after a roll call. On this the vote stood, 35 ayes and 47 nays. The vote then came on the open ballot as reported by the minority. Every Payne man voting aye, and every Anti-Payne man voting nay.

Those who voted for an open ballot were: Godfrey, Lewis, Myers, O'Neal, Read and Van Cleaf of the Senate, and Addison, Buchanan, Byal, Cole, Crites, Finley, Goodman, Hull, Higgins, Kahle, Marsh,

Myers, Stillwell, Shultz, Sharp, Weldy, Work, Young of Adams, and Young of Marion, of the House. Total, 25. Those who voted against an open ballot, were Senators Brenner, Caldwell, Cable, Crowell, Elliott, Jaeger, Levering, McLyman, O'Brien, Pruden, Ramey, Smith, Welch, Williams, Williston and White, and the members of the House were Bargar, Bohl, Brunner, Bruce, Baker, Beatty, Black, Cunningham, Cosgrove, Cogan, Cummings, Cuff, Edwards, Francisco, Fierce, George, Holbrook, Harbaugh, Hunt, Habbeler, Hamilton, Johnson, Lowenstein, Lisle, Mooney, Menke, Malone, McBride, Poe, Roche, Puckerin, Staubach, Stalter, Stevenson, Stauffer, Thompson of Hamilton, Thompson of Knox, Wolf, Turner, Young of Franklin, Zeigler. Total, 57.

This vote foreshadowed the result. The profoundest silence prevailed during the proceedings, broken only by the clerk's voice, or some of the impatient crowd on the outside hammering on the doors. The sound echoed through the hall with startling effect, and recalled Macduff thundering at the castle gate, after Macbeth had killed the king. Rushing from the presence of the awful crime, he exclaimed:

> "O horror! horror!! horror!!! Tongue nor heart
> Cannot conceive nor name thee!"

Every man present felt that an awful crime was being committed. Over half of them knew that they were guilty agents, accessory before the fact—paid participants in the act—betraying the people—and selling for a price that which they had but the day before solemnly sworn, with hands uplifted, to guard and protect, namely, the Constitution and the laws and rights of the people. It is no wonder that some trembled and looked nervously and wretchedly about. That sound at the door aroused visions of an angry and an outraged people. It was ominous. Had some Macduff rushed upon the scene and cried murder and treason, the conspirators would have fled. As it was, the task was left to the conscience of each man, and it thundered so softly, that the crime was hastened to its consummation.

The majority report was adopted by 57 ayes and 25 nays. The roll was called upon this vote, and it was used as the pay-roll in settling the accounts and making the final payments. The names of the candidates were presented without speeches. Senator Williams, of Cleveland, presented the name of Henry B. Payne. Senator John O'Neil, of Zanesville, presented the name of Geo. H. Pendleton, and from a dark corner in the hall, where he sat by himself as though he feared the light, Senator Geo. Elliott, of Butler, arose and faintly whispered the name of General Durbin Ward. Bohl of Washington, Cogan of Hamilton, and Jaeger of Ottawa, acted as tellers. Mr. Bohl, of Washington, moved that the roll be called and each one pledge himself to support the nominee. This blundering and ill-advised motion conveyed an imputation that aroused a storm of indignant protest.

This zealous henchman had taken one step too much, and frightened at his own indiscretion, Mr. Bohl quickly recalled his motion. The result of the ballot was as follows: Those who voted for Ward were, Senators Reed, Van Cleaf and Williston; and members of the House: Byal, Edwards, Johnson, Higgins, Habbeler, Marsh, McBride, Puckerin, Turner, Work, Young of Adams, Young of Marion, and Schultz. Total 17.

Those who voted for Pendleton, were Senators Godfrey, Lewis, Myers, O'Neil; and members of the House were: Addison, Buchanan, Cole, Crites, Finley, Goodman, Hull, Kahle, Stillwell, Sharp, Weldy. Total 15. Mr. Stevenson voted for Geddes, and Mr. Myers voted for Booth.

Those who voted for Payne were: Senators Brenner, Caldwell, Cable, Crowell, Elliott, Jaeger, Levering, McLyman, O'Brien, Pruden, Ramey, Smith, Welch, Williams and White; and members of the House were: Bargar, Bohl, Brunner, Bruce, Baker, Beatty, Black, Cunningham, Cosgrove, Cogan, Cummings, Cuff, Francisco, Fierce, George, Holbrook, Harbaugh, Hamilton, Hunt, Lowenstein, Lisle, Mooney, Menke, Malone, Poe, Roche, Stalter, Stauffer, Thompson of Hamilton, Thompson of Knox, Wolf and Young of Franklin, and Zeigler. Total 48.

Mr. Elmer White then made the announcement which confirmed the sale of the Senatorship to Hon. Henry B. Payne and its purchase by the Standard Oil

Company. The ballots were all carefully preserved and turned over to Jno. R. McLean, who carefully put the same away in his safe, for future reference. It was with difficulty that Mr. Oliver Payne restrained the exuberance and hilarity of his personal and paid followers. He knew that it would not do to be too brutal in rejoicing over the purchase, as the deed had not yet been consummated and ratified. Mr. John R. McLean was not so considerate. He was wildly delirious over the result. Not only had Mr. Pendleton, his own and his father's foe, been defeated, but he had been humiliated; never had there been such a piece of refined diabolism in the history of politics, as had been executed against Mr. Pendleton. When the Bosses knew that they had votes to spare for Mr. Payne, at the urgent solicitation of Mr. McLean, Mr. Oliver Payne kindly consented to loan him a few, and these were selected from counties that were known to be very strong against Mr. Payne, and they were instructed to vote for Mr. Ward, so that his vote might be larger than Mr. Pendleton's. If the reader will compare the list of those who voted for and against the open ballot, with the vote for Senator, he can easily pick out these men.

XII. It is not claimed that all of the men who voted for Mr. Payne received a money consideration. A majority of them did. Several who voted for Mr. Payne did so at the solicitation of others who were paid. To some extent they were ignorant and innocent. The money expended up to the election, Jan. 15, 1884, was in the neighborhood of $300,000. This may now be looked upon as the fixed market price of the Senatorship in Ohio, unless there should be open competition in the market, when prices might go up.

One of the most peculiar features of this contest, was the fact that some ten or dozen members who had been elected as the champions of labor, were among the most pliant and useful tools of the greatest and worst monopoly of all, and the first trust, The Standard Oil Company. Every workingman, so-called, on the Democratic side, voted against an open ballot, and every one of them were in favor of Mr. Payne, except Addison, of Muskingum. It is a case of the extremes meeting. In the language of the Supreme Court of Ohio, in deciding a case and commenting on the methods of the Standard Oil Company, we might add, "How peculiar!" when we see that those champions who have been chosen to combat the dangerous tendencies of trusts, are the first to yield to the blandishments of monopoly and money, and are apparently its easiest and cheapest victims.

XIII. Those who did not sell their votes were not forgotten, when a national Democratic administration came into power. President Cleveland and Senator Payne entered upon their official careers on March 4, 1885. Among the first men appointed to office were the Payne men in the "Coal Oil Legislature." The three, McLyman, Bargar and Crowell, who made the majority report to the caucus, were appointed to Federal positions. Mr. McLyman got an office in Toledo, and an "old horse from Oliver Payne, and nothing more." Mr. G. H. Bargar was made pension agent at Columbus, and Mr. Crowell was sent as consul to a station in Siam. Senator Caldwell was made collector of the port in Cincinnati, and Mr. Riley, who was chairman of Mr. McLean's Highland House Convention, was made postmaster at Cincinnati. Senator Elliott was appointed a government agent, and Senator Jaeger, and a number of members of the House, notably Messrs. Bohl and Bruce, were appointed to Federal places. Hon. A. R. Van Cleaf, who signed the minority report in favor of an open ballot and voted for Durbin Ward, has several times been presented as a suitable person for a Federal appointment, but has never been successful. Mr. Van Cleaf has long been the editor of one of the leading Democratic weeklies of Ohio, the Circleville *Democrat and Watchman*. Its columns have never been for sale, and the integrity of its editor has never been questioned, either in public or private life. His character as an honest man and a Democrat, who is not for sale, having been firmly established, it constituted sufficient reason for his exclusion from the emoluments of office. Such a man cannot be tempted by "Boodle," nor used by the "Bosses," and if every editor in Ohio, of whatever political convictions, were as faithful to their life mission and work, in the greatest of all professions known under our form of government, there would be an end to "Bosses and Boodle in Ohio Politics."

SANTA CLAUS BRICE FILLING THE LEGISLATIVE STOCKINGS.

(*Porcupine, Dec. 1889.*)

CHAPTER X.

THE TRAIL OF THE SERPENT.—THE DOLLAR MARK RAMPANT ON THE ESCUTCHEON OF OHIO.—BRICE DUPLICATES THE PAYNE PURCHASE.

LIBERTY and monopoly can not live together. What chance have we against the persistent coming and the easy coalescence of the confederated cliques, which aspire to say of all business, "This belongs to us," and whose members, though moving among us as brothers, are using against us, through the corporate forms we have given them, powers of invisibility of entail and accumulation, unprecedented because impersonal and immortal, and most peculiar of all, power to act as persons, as in the commission of crimes, with the exemption from punishment as persons? Two classes study and practice politics and government—place hunters and privilege hunters. In a world of relativities like ours, size of area has a great deal to do with the truth of principles. America has grown so big—and the tickets to be voted and the powers of goverment, and the duties of citizens, and the profits of personal and public functions have all grown so big—that the average citizen has broken down. No man can half understand or half operate the fulness of this big citizenship, except by giving his whole time to it. This the place hunter can do, and the privilege hunter. Government, therefore—municipal, state, national—is passing into the hands of these two classes, specialized for the functions of power by their appetite for the fruits of power. The power of citizenship is relinquished by those who do not and cannot know how to exercise it to those who can—and do—by those who have a livelihood to make to those who make politics their livelihood.

These specialists of the ward club, the primary, the campaign, the election, and office unite, by a law as irresistible as that of the sexes, with those who want all the goods of governments—charters, contracts, rulings, permits. From this marriage it is easy to imagine that among some other people than ourselves, and in some other century than this, the offspring might be the most formidable, elusive, unrestrained, impersonal, and cruel tyranny the world has yet seen. There might come a time when the policemen and the railroad president would equally show that they cared nothing for the citizen, individually or collectively, because aware that they and not he were the government. Certainly such an attempt to corner "the dear people" and the earth and the fulness thereof will break down. It is for us to decide whether we will let it go on till it breaks down of itself, dragging down to die, as a savage dies of his vice, the civilization it has gripped with its hundred hands; or whether, while we are still young, still virtuous, we will break it down, self-consciously as the civilized man, reforming, crushes down the evil. If we cannot find a remedy, all that we love in the word America must die.

It will be an awful price to pay if this attempt at government of the people, by the people, for the people, must perish from off the face of the earth to prove to mankind that the political brotherhood cannot survive where industrial brotherhood is denied. But the demonstration is worth even that.—*Henry D. Loydd, in Wealth Against Comonwealth.*

"We've all struck oil," yelled an enthusiast, when the result of the Standard Oil caucus was announced! After the election of Henry B. Payne in joint session, Wednesday, July 16, the Journal of the House showed the following proceedings.

Mr. Love offered the following resolution:

H. R. No. 24: WHEREAS, The press of the state and reputable men of both political parties have openly charged that bribery and corruption have been resorted to, and successfully practiced in securing the election of Hon. Henry B. Payne, as United States Senator from Ohio, and that members of the House of Representatives of the 66th General Assembly have solicited and received bribes for their votes for United States Senator; therefore,

Resolved, That the Speaker appoint a select committee of five, to make a full and complete investigation of said alleged charges of bribery and corruption, and that said committee shall have power to send for persons, books and papers, and shall report to the House at the earliest date practicable.

Mr. Bohl gave notice of his intention to discuss.

Mr. Love moved that the rules be suspended, that the resolution may be discussed now.

Which was agreed to.

The question being on the adoption of the resolution—

Mr. Myers moved to amend the resolution by inserting after the preamble the following:

"AND WHEREAS, It is charged by newspapers and other irresponsible parties, that one Charles Foster, late Governor of Ohio, has corruptly expended money to debauch the voters of Ohio, and corruptly secure the votes of candidates for the Legislature to vote for him for United States Senator in the event of their election and a Republican Legislature being chosen, and to secure his nomination and election for Governor; therefore,

Be it resolved, That said committee be authorized to investigate all said charges, beginning with the nomination of said Foster in Cincinnati in 1879, until the present time, and charges relating thereto or any other subject that may be called to their attention; said investigation shall be full, thorough and complete, and the committee shall employ stenographers to make full reports of all their proceedings, and said committee may meet here or elsewhere, and shall always sit with open doors."

Mr. Jones raised the point of order, that the amendment was out of order, inasmuch as the matter contained therein was not germane to the resolution.

Which point of order the Speaker decided was not well taken.

The question being on agreeing to the amendment—

Mr. Sheppard moved to amend the amendments by adding the following:

"And whereas, it is publicly charged that one Allen O. Myers obtained his nomination for a candidate for member of this Sixty-sixth General Assembly by stuffing the ballot-box; therefore, said committee shall also fully investigate said charges, and shall report the result of the same to this House."

Which was agreed to, Mr. Myers accepting the amendment.

The question being on agreeing to the amendment as amended, it was agreed to.

The question now being on the adoption of the resolution as amended, the yeas and nays were taken, and resulted—yeas 35, nays 52, as follows:

Yeas—Messrs. Brown, Cunningham, Deyo, Dickson, Farrar, Fierce, Ford, Gest, Greiner, Hughes, Hunt, Johnson of Huron, Johnson of Williams, Laird, Lantz, Loewenstein, Love, Malone, Matthews, Mooney, Myers, Peet, Primrose, Rarey, Roche, Ross, Sackett, Sheppard, Stilwell, Striker, Washburn, Wilson, Work, Young of Adams, and Young of Franklin—35.

Nays—Messrs. Addison, Baker, Bargar, Beatty, Black, Bohl, Bruce, Brunner, Buchanan, Burnett, Cole, Cosgrove, Cummings, Edwards, Emerson, Finley, Francisco, Gaston, George, Goodman, Habbeler, Hadley, Haley, Harbaugh, Higgins, Hilles, Holbrook, Jones, Kahle, Linduff, Lisle, Lyman, McBride, Menke, Miles, Murray, Ogden, Poe, Puckrin, Schultz, Sherman, Stalter, Stanbery, Staubach, Stevenson, Thorp, Turner, Walker, Wolf, Young of Marion, Ziegler, and Speaker—52.

So the resolution was lost.

Thirteen Democrats and twenty-two Republicans voted for an investigation, and thirty-five Democrats and seventeen Republicans voted against an exposure. The Boodlers of both parties were opposed to investigations. They are useless and expensive. Some honest men voted no, because they believed such an investigation would be a farce. Some Democratic members who had been hired, voted for an investigation in order to assume a virtue in the eyes of the people that they did not possess.

The excitement and corruption of the Senatorial sale, as usual, left the Legislature utterly demoralized, and unfit, if not incapacitated, for a proper and faithful discharge of their duties. If there were no other good and sufficient reason for the election of the United States Senator by the people, the demoralization of the Legislature, which follows such corrupt conflict as preceded Mr. Payne's purchase of the office, is a conclusive and overwhelming one.

Suspicious bills of various kinds made their appearance in both houses. Among these was an innocent measure by Mr. Kohler of Summit. This bill is what is called a "milker"—a Jersey cow driven into the Legislative pasture at one end, for the members to milk before it reached the other. H. B. No. 177. By Mr. Kohler, "supplementary to Sec. 3880," was introduced in the House, Thursday, January 31. This bill in connection with the methods employed at the Senatorial election, gave the name of "Coil Oil" to this Legislature. The Constitution plainly provides, that every bill shall have its purpose plainly set forth in its title. When this provision is not complied with, there is always ground for suspicion. Mr. Kohler is a lawyer, has since been Attorney General, and is now a candidate for Judge in the Akron district, and he can explain how, as a lawyer, he came to introduce a bill that failed to comply with the plain requirements of the Constitution as to its title. The bill was referred to the Judiciary Committee, and on Feb. 28, it was reported, and its passage recommended by six members of the committee. It was placed upon the calendar and came up for consideration March 7, and was recommitted to the Judiciary Committee for some mysterious purposes on motion of Mr. Hadley of Fayette. The record don't show how it got out of the committee. It probably crawled out over the transom much to the surprise of the members. On April 3, on motion of Mr. Cole of Stark, the innocent bill was lassoed and made a special order for Wednesday, April 9. The bill came up on that day. The previous question was demanded by Mr. Sharp of Holmes. The bill was put upon its passage and lost by a vote of 45 ayes to 36 nays. It required 53 votes to pass the House. On Thursday, April 10, the vote by which the bill was lost, was reconsidered on motion of Mr. Weldy of Hocking, who had voted against it, and the bill passed by a vote of 63 to 15. It was sent to the Senate, and Mr. Elmer White, of Defiance, as President *pro tem.*, was in the chair, and waiting for the bill. He seemed to be possessed of important information upon this particular measure, and he received it and locked it up in his desk, and did not present it to the Senate until Monday, April 14, the day the Legislature adjourned. For several days the bill was lost, which caused scandal and excitement, but at the proper time it was produced by Mr. White, but it was dead. It was never heard of at the next session. It was a bill to authorize a pipe line to be constructed from the Pennsylvania oil fields to Cleveland, in opposition to the Standard Oil Company. If this was its object, it was a most commendable one, but strange to say its author did not urge its passage at the next session and it was never heard of again. Its worthy author and the members of the Judiciary Committee and the House, had been imposed upon by some wicked person, who had dipped his hands in the golden grease at the Senatorial election, and he was trying to make the Standard Oil Company disgorge.

II. Gov. Hoadly's administration was in keeping with the scandalous acts attending the Payne purchase. He gave the best offices in his gift to men who had been conspicuous in the Payne camp and canvass. Archbishop Alex. Sands was the guardian angel of Mr. Hoadly's administration. You could hardly get in or out of the Governor's office without encountering Mr. Sands. He seemed to ooze from the walls in the most mysterious and unaccountable manner. Where he came from and how he always got there, nobody knew, but what he was there for a great many guessed at. When all is revealed on that last great day, we may be able to learn the secret ties that bound George Hoadly, a reformed Democrat, to Alexander Cassius Sands, a deformed Boss and Boodler. The leading attorney of the liquor dealers association had become Governor of Ohio, but he added nothing to a former good name and high character. He conducted the Governor's office upon the same level that had characterized Gov. Foster's administration. He acted as though he had purchased the property and he had a right to do as he pleased with his own. All his efforts were directed toward building up a personal following to further his own ambition. Mr. Hoadly and Mr. McLean were as loving as brothers.

The compact made the year before was still in force, and binding on both. At the state convention held June, 1884, Allen G. Thurman, Durbin Ward, Geo. Hoadly and Jno. R. McLean were chosen delegates at large to the Democratic National Convention, which met July 8, in Chicago. Mr. J. R. McLean was chosen chairman of the delegation, and those he could control by purchase or persuasion, opposed Allen G. Thurman as a candidate for President, and supported Gov. Hoadly. It was a pitiable spectacle, fully as disgraceful as the performance at Cincinnati four years before. Allen G. Thurman attended the convention, and was received by a sincere and affectionate demonstration, that proved the warm place he occupied in the hearts of the people. Wm. P. Thompson and other agents of the Standard Oil Company were on hand, helping Mr. McLean to destroy Mr. Thurman. The scandal attending the purchase of the Senatorship, had killed off Mr. Payne forever, as a political quantity of any kind. Judge Thurman's name was presented to the convention by one of the Breckinridges, a son of Jno. C., a family famous for its eloquent and gifted sons. It was received by the convention and the galleries, in a manner that denoted strength, if there could only be unity in the Ohio delegation. Hon. T. E. Powell presented the name of Geo. Hoadly, and it was received with a coldness and indifference, that was painful when compared with the warm reception given Mr. Thurman. Gov. Hoadly's candidacy was properly looked upon as an act of treason to his state and party. One ballot settled the contest and showed up Gov. Hoadly in a humiliating manner. Out of 721 votes, Geo. Hoadly got 3, one from Louisiana and 2 from Ohio. Mr. Cleveland was nominated, receiving 392, which was made unanimous. Mr. Thurman got 88 votes. Of the 46 votes in the Ohio delegation, Mr. Thurman got 23, Mr. Cleveland 21, and Mr. Hoadly 2. Gov. Hoadly telegraphed that Ohio would give a Democratic majority.

The result in Ohio was: Blaine, 400,082; Cleveland, 368,280; Prohibitionists, 11,069; Labor, 5,179; and scattering, 2,549. Total, 787,159. The largest vote ever polled in the state. Had it not been for the infamy of the Standard Oil's purchase of the Senatorship, Ohio would have gone Democratic. But this outrage prepared the way, and in a measure justified the use of the armed marshals, and the federal machinery at Cincinnati and other points in the state, which to some extent influenced the result in favor of the Republicans, as there was a falling off in the Democratic vote of 12,000 between the October and the November elections, and an increase of the Republican vote. It is an unusual thing in the Presidential election in Ohio, for the head of the state ticket to poll more votes than the Presidential candidate of the party, but in 1884, Mr. Newman, the Democratic candidate for Secretary of State, polled 380,355 votes in October, and in November Mr. Cleveland polled 368,280 votes.

IV. A chain of calamities marked the advent of Gov. Hoadly's administration and followed in the wake of the scandalous crimes of the Senatorial election, apparently as a natural sequence. There was flood, famine and suffering in the Ohio Valley, and riot, killings and fire in Cincinnati. The violation of law and the outraging of public decency by the law makers, brought an immediate echo from the masses, and they became law breakers, and the burning of the court house at Cincinnati and the killing wounding of many citizens, was a lesson that has gone unheeded, and we are destined to see many similar scenes of blood and destruction in the not far distant future.

There were still ominous signs during the winter of 1885 that the crimes committed in the purchase of the Senatorship by the Standard Oil Company, had neither been forgotten nor forgiven by the people of Ohio. As Mr. Cleveland entered the White House, Henry B. Payne entered the United States Senate. One of his first and most pleasing duties was to vote for his own son-in-law and a brother-in-law of the Standard Oil Company, Mr. Wm. C. Whitney, of New York, for Secretary of the Navy. The great trust had grown so strong, that it was now looking for wider fields of action to display its powers, and increase its gains. It had chained as captives to its triumphant car, all the industrial forces on the land, and made them and the people pay tribute, and it now sought to enslave the freedom of the seas. The sequel shows that this mighty master has made a great beginning. But let us be thankful to God and the Standard Oil Company, that we are still permitted to breathe the air without tax, although the gases from the distillation of the Standard Oil begin to poison it.

Without his knowledge, Mr. Cleveland, to some extent, owed his nomination and election as President of the United States, to the "silent and abhorrent forces" of the Standard Oil Company. Wm. P. Thompson, a Republican and one of the leading officials of the corporation, was at Chicago, and gave his personal influence and aid to Mr. Wm. C. Whitney and others, in securing Mr. Cleveland's nomination.

Owing to Mr. Whitney's prominence and influence in New York politics, but not because of his relations to the Standard Oil Compady, Mr. Cleveland felt constrained to give him a place in his official family, and with a representative in the Senate and the Cabinet, the Standard Oil Company entered upon its career of universal conquest.

V. In 1885, the Ohio Republicans re-nominated Joseph B. Foraker for Governor, and the Democrats re-nominated Geo. Hoadly. The latter would like to have had a place in the Cabinet, but Mr. Cleveland had no use for the Ohio man. Gov. Hoadly's ambition had been eclipsed by the success of the son of New York, and he had become utterly disgusted with himself, and thoroughly sickened with politics, and he was not as eager to secure the Democratic nomination as he had been two years before. He did not fancy the contest. Defeat seemed certain, and the records and scandals of the state administration, the Payne purchase and the "Coil Oil Legislature," made a burden too great for any party or candidate to carry and succeed. But Jno. R. McLean was a candidate for the Senatorship against John Sherman, and he and the Standard Oil Company gave liberally to the campaign fund, and the contest was a memorable one. Every inch of ground was disputed by both parties, and the result was a Republican victory.

The vote was impressively large, and justified the charges of fraud made by both parties. The total vote was 733,967, the largest vote ever polled outside of a presidential year. Hoadly got 341,095, Foraker 359,281, Prohibitionists 28,982, Labor 2,016, scattering 2,832. Hoadly had polled 18,000 votes less than he had received two years before, and Foraker had polled 12,000 votes more.

The Republicans had a majority of one on joint

ballot, and John Sherman was re-elected United States Senator. The uncertainty as to the Legislature, kept the state in a state of uproar for several weeks. The most outrageous frauds had been committed in Cincinnati, and were charged to Mr. John R. McLean, and when the Legislature met, the McLean delegation from Hamilton County was promptly unseated in the House, and later the same was done in the Senate.

In Franklin County two candidates on the Democratic ticket, Messrs Myers and Young, were beaten by the open opposition of Mr. Thurman's friends. After the election and before the count was completed, the official returns were taken out of the safe on Sunday and a number of votes, (over 200) were added to those recorded as having been cast for the Democratic candidates. This forgery was replaced in the safe on Sunday night, and when the Canvassing Board met on Monday to complete its labors, the crime was promptly discovered by Mr. John Joyce, who, as county clerk, was the president of the canvassers, and seemed to be expecting it. The fraud was so evident, bungling and senseless, that it was immediately thrown out. This forgery and discovery created great excitement all over Ohio, and showed that the people were in no humor to tamely submit to another outrage upon the purity of elections, that would send another millionaire, Boss and Boodler to the United States Senate. An effort was made to send the Boss and his tools to the penitentiary. The big fish jumped over the seine and escaped. They caught one or two minnows.

The forgery in Columbus was wrongfully laid at the door of Mr. John ~~R.~~ McLean. The people, in looking for the responsible party, very properly located it near one who must not only have a motive for the commission of the crime, but the money and power to induce its perpetration. Mr. McLean wanted to go to the United States Senate. That was the motive. He was a candidate, and had the money and power, and this combination was conclusive evidence in the excited public mind, that Mr. McLean was the criminal. But let us give the devil his due. There was one Democratic vote short in the Legislature, and this chasm lay between Mr. McLean and his ambition. He had his agents out looking diligently for that vote, but they never found it. Had the forgery in Columbus been successful and been counted, it would not have elected a member of the Legislature. The next highest candidate, Mr. Young, would have been beaten 39 votes. The prosecuting attorney and the sheriff only would have been elected. There is no doubt but that if a Democratic member could have secured a certificate of election by fraud, that Mr. McLean would have been willing to pay for it, but it is an insult to his keen business sense, and his character as a shrewd man in money matters, to suppose that he paid for something he did not get. It is said he gave $10,000 for the commission of this crime, and when it was done, if counted, it would not have accomplished what he so ardently wished. It is said "that there is honor among thieves," but it may be set down as an axiom for the study of philosophers, and as a guide for the young and innocent, who may be tempted into the flowery paths of politics, that there is absolutely no honor among politicians. Where ambition and personal interests are at stake, a politician will sacrifice honor (if he has any), friendship, principle, party, everything that men hold sacred, to defeat a rival, punish an enemy, or advance himself. In the politician's garden, promises, rank and fragrant, bloom on every bush, but these beautiful blossoms rarely ripen into performance. Perhaps there was never a crime committed, around which clustered so much perjury, rascality, treachery, bribery, double-dealing and cross purposes, as distinguished the famous or rather infamous Columbus tally-sheet figures of 1885. The field of fiction does not afford an equal. The mind of man cannot conceive such turpitude as was displayed, but which was never revealed. It would take a volume to give the details, and a master to properly portray the plans and purposes of the two leading characters. We may be the one chosen for this work, but this is not the place. There were three forgeries committed. The one discovered was committed in the pententiary by a convict, on the original tally-sheet. The others were used to cover sinister purposes, arouse suspicions, involve the innocent and implicate John R. McLean. The first was intended to prevent him from going to the United States Senate. All accomplished the designs of a talented and magnificent scoundrel.

VI. Gov. Hoadly stepped down and out from the Governor's office, returned to Cincinnati, "received a reception," and resumed the practice of a profession in which he was once an ornament. But he did not seem to be a happy man. He acted like one with a burden on his soul, which he could not roll off. In 1887 he determined to remove to New York City. Feb. 26, 1887, he was tendered a farewell banquet by citizens at the Young Men's Democratic Club at Cincinnati. He made a speech in which he bid farewell to Ohio and all of his political hopes, and as if on his political deathbed, he made this confession, in the absence of Archbishop Sands, his father confessor: "Letting the past alone and turning to the future, the duty of the Democracy is this: Let it be known that when a rascal is nominated for office on the Democratic ticket, he is not a Democratic candidate for office; that when nominations are bought and sold, they are not Democratic nominations, and where dishonest methods are resorted to, the promoters of the fraud are to be pursued, even into the penitentiary, where they belong."

We can hardly deny admiration to Marc Antony, when he stands over the bloody corse of Cæsar and shakes the dice of presumption for an empire, by producing the will of the "late lamented," and bribes the mob by a tearful announcement that Cæsar has given to the people and "to their heirs forever," the parks and property he had stolen from them and could not take with him. Our posterity in Ohio should lift their eyes, overflowing with melting gratitude, to George Hoadly, for his last will and testament to the "New Democracy," in which he points out the way to recover that which he helped to rob it of, and if the corpse will permit it, when the statue to Durbin Ward is completed, George Hoadly's plea for purity in politics should be graven in brass on the pedestal.

VII. The crimes against the ballot in the contest of 1885, aroused the public and resulted in the enactment of a series of laws to preserve the "purity of elections." In January, 1886, the Cincinnati *Commercial Gazette* opened up the scandal of the Payne purchase, by giving the names of members of the Legislature and amounts that had been paid each for their votes. The Ohio House of Representatives appointed a committee of five, to make an investigation. Fifty-five witnesses were called. Three of the committee, Messrs Rawlins, Cowgill and Thompson, Republicans, found that "Bribery is not easily proven. Our laws make the giver and taker of a bribe equally guilty, and visit both by the same penalty, which is doubtless just, but the effect of which is to bind the guilty parties together in a bond of secrecy, which neither can break without imperiling his own liberty.

When the crime has been determined upon and committed deliberately, the parties thereto will adopt every means to conceal it; not only such ingenuity as is exercised by criminals in the preparation and commission of crime, but perjury as well, to prevent its discovery, so that it is only by circumstantial evidence, by unguarded and unintentional admissions, or by the sudden and undue acquisition of property, and other significant circumstances, and rarely by direct evidence that the charge can be proved."

The committee found nobody guilty, and mildly recommended that the evidence be sent to the United States Senate, for such action as "it might deem advisable." This was done. The Ohio House resolved "that ample testimony was adduced to warrant the belief that the seat of Henry B. Payne, in the United States Senate, was purchased by corrupt use of money." The Ohio Senate charged, "that the election was procured by the corrupt use of money and by other corrupt means and practices." Both Houses, the Executive and the Republican press of Ohio, demanded an investigation by the United States Senate. But the Senate refused to investigate. "How peculiar?" How much did it cost to suppress the investigation in Ohio and at Washington? Had the investigation been ordered, there would have been quite an exodus of millionaires and Standard Oil people to Europe.

Four Senators, Pugh, Saulsbury, Vance and Eustis,

voted against investigation, and Hoar and Frye voted for it. Senator Hoar said the Senate seemed to be indifferent as "to whether its seats are to be in the future the subject of bargain and sale, or may be presented by a few millionaires as a compliment to a friend." In the debate he said: "A refusal to investigate will be the most unfortunate fact in the history of the Senate."

The Senate refused to order an investigation, and when the vote was announced, Senator Edmunds said: "This is a day of infamy for the Senate of the United States." But this great body, that was invented to check the honest passion of the people, has put in so many of these kinds of days, of recent years, that one don't count.

With the announcement of the result, the Standard Oil conspirators and its allies and tools breathed easier. It had escaped again, but it was a hard and expensive job, and a narrow escape. In debate, a year or so later, Mr. Payne opened his month for the first time, and indignantly denied that any member of the Standard Oil Company had used money to buy votes for him for Senator. During all the charges for years, he remained silent. An honest man would have resented the charges, challenged investigation and spurned the office. In this speech, unfortunately, after denying that money had been used by the Standard Oil Company to secure his election, he stated that members of the company always gave liberally to the campaign fund, and he said the company used money to beat him for Congress in 1874. When nominated, he promised his people to return with clean hands and a heart undefiled.

May 16, 1876, Mr. Hopkins, of the Pittsburgh, Pa., district, offered a resolution to create a committee of five to investigate the "peculiar" methods by which many industries were being crippled by freight discrimination by the railroads. "I object!" came from a member near him, and the resolution failed. Looking around, Mr. Hopkins saw that objection had been made by a venerable looking gentlemen with a priestly cast of countenance. It was the father-in-law and the father of the Standard Oil Company, Henry B. Payne. He was willing that an investigation should be made by the Standing Committee on Commerce. An investigation was ordered, begun and dropped dead in its tracks, and some one stole the evidence.

When the bill to create the Inter-state Commerce Commission, to prevent discrimination in freight and and other abuses, came up for final passage, Mr. Payne voted to indefinitely postpone, and when this failed, he voted against its passage. He boldly championed the Standard Oil Company in one of the few speeches he made in the Senate. He said: "The Standard Oil Company is a remarkable and a wonderful institution. It has accomplished within the last twenty years, as a commercial enterprise, what no other company or association of modern times has accomplished." No one conversant with the facts will dispute the statement of Mr. Payne.

The Secretary of the Navy, Mr. Whitney, began to rehabilitate the American navy. This prepared the way for the advent of the Standard Oil on the high seas. Experience has proven, that if you pour oil to the windward, it soothes the waves.

In the winter of 1891, Congress passed a postal subsidy law, to pay a higher rate of compensation for carrying the mails under our flag, in American ships, made out of American material by American mechanics, and to be manned by American sailors. This was an expensive but a patriotic measure, and the American people are always willing to pay a little extra if the band will play "Yankee Doodle." It did, and we are now paying the piper.

In March, 1891, Mr. Windom, secretary of the treasury, died suddenly, and President Harrison named Charles Foster, of Ohio, to fill the vacancy. There was some opposition to his confirmation in the Senate, and Senator Henry B. Payne was quite active in securing votes enough to insure Mr. Foster's confirmation. The Standard Oil Company was the tie that bound this Democrat and Republican together. This was the last manifestation of activity in Mr. Payne's official life, as he was succeeded on March 4, 1891, by "the smartest man in America," Calvin Steward Brice, of Ohio and New York. Nothing had been done under the Postal subsidy law of 1891. It seemed to be dead, but it was only sleeping. In May, 1892, a bill went through both houses like greased lightning. This bill set forth that if any vessel, of a certain build, and already in existence, would comply with the law, it might carry the mails and receive the subsidy. There were only two vessels that met the requirements of this sudden and "peculiar" law, the "City of New York" and the "City of Paris," belonging to the Inman Line, and owned by the Standard Oil Company. The International Steamship Company was formed, and the Postmaster General awarded it the contracts for carrying the mails, two years before the old contract expired. That is, in 1893 a contract for ten years was made, from 1895 to 1905. Why this haste! The government of the United States bound itself to pay $4 a mile, for 52 trips a year, between New York and Southampton, of 3162 miles each, for ten years, to the International Standard Oil Company, and the same rate was made, for the same time, with the same Company, for the same number of trips, between New York and Antwerp, being $1,354,496 a year paid by the government to this company for carrying mails alone, on a capital of $10,000,000 actually invested.

This tremendous advantage creates an absolute monopoly by the favor of the government and with the money of the people, and gives this organization such an advantage as to destroy all competition, and drive all rival lines between the United States and Europe, from the high seas. As a commerce destroyer, the Confederate privateers cannot compare. The only thing American about the first two ships was the flag, and the dividends. Secretary of Treasury Foster issued an order, abrogating the law requiring Americans to be employed on these ships, and they are officered and manned by British, and when an American applies for a place, he is laughed at and ordered ashore. A congressional report made in 1874, shows that the Pacific Mail Company spent $700,000 to get a similar job through Congress. Before we bid a final farewell to Mr. Payne as a Senator, by right of purchase, we wish to call attention to another act, that shows how disinterested was his course in his purchased seat. At the session of 1889, upon the urgent representations of the Secretary of the Navy, $1,000,000 was appropriated to buy nickel ore, to use as an alloy to temper steel for armour plates for our new Navy. Congress took the tariff off of nickel for the same reason. The leading nickel mine was in Sudberry, Canada. The Standard Oil Company owned this mine, and got the appropriation and the tariff taken off of nickel. The ore was held back for a year, and on April 1, 1890, there was 5,000 tons of ore ready for shipment, and the tariff on this at the old rate would amount to $1,500,000. A suit disclosed the fact that Henry B. Payne was a stockholder in the Canadian Copper Company, which had a contract with the Secretary of the Navy to furnish nickel. "How peculiar!" We agree with Mr. Payne, "The Standard Oil Company is a wonderful organization." Mr. Bissell, the Democatic Postmaster General when the subsidy went into effect in 1895, was one of the attorneys at Buffalo, in 1886, that defended the Standard Oil Company conspirators, for bribing an employee to blow up an oil refinery, to destroy a rival in business. He is now being mentioned as a candidate to fill the vacancy on the supreme bench of the United States, caused by the death of Judge Jackson.

VII. Mr. Foster, after an absence from public life of six years, has appeared upon the scene as Secretary of the Treasury. He comes blithesome and gay, as a milkmaid, hand in hand with his pupil and prodigy, Calvin S. Brice. As a Boss and a Boodler in Ohio Politics, Mr. Brice ranks as the rankest. He is a colossus. It does not seem possible, as we gaze upon this monster of modern industrial conditions, that Mr. Brice ever went through the vulgar routine by which humanity make their advent upon the troubled scenes of life, but he frankly assures the world, in a biographical sketch, prepared by his secretary and approved by himself, that that momentous event in his career occurred at Denmark, Canaan Township, Morrow County, (but then a part of Marion County, O.) on Sept. 17, 1845. Mr. Brice's father, Rev. Wm. K. Brice, came to Ohio in 1840 from Maryland. Mr. Brice is the first Boss and Boodler of any prominence in Ohio, who descended from "the people to the South." In another biographical sketch with a wood cut, both of which were paid for, we are told that "Mr. Brice stands high as a man of large capacity in affairs, *generous* in disposition, of singular mental alertness, and electric in action." This is too good to be lost in an obscure volume of uncertain circulation, and for the benefit of Mr. Brice and posterity we reproduce it here, where it will live, free of charge. No blame should attach to young Brice because his father was a minister. His subsequent career shows that he has nobly surmounted the prejudice and difficulties that are supposed to surround a "preacher's boy." He was going to school at Oxford, O., when the war broke out. He was a very busy young man during the war. He graduated from college, taught school, enlisted three times, in three years, in three different regiments, and found time while putting down the war to attend the Vallandingham convention at Columbus in 1863. This information we find in several biographies or autobiographies, and the fact that at seventeen he offered his services "for the suppression of the rebellion," stamps him as a remarkable young man. After putting down the rebellion with a bloodless valor that Mr. Whitelaw Reed honors with a considerate silence, in his "Ohio in the War," Mr. Brice studied and was admitted to the practice of law. He located in Lima, O., and played poker and waited for clients. His patron, Charles Fostor, relates, that when Mr. Brice formed a law partnership, he and his new partner were both Republican in politics, and at Mr. Brice's suggestion he tossed a copper to see which should be the Democrat in the firm. Mr. Brice lost, and the Democratic party of Ohio unconsciously won this brazen prize and its future Boss and master.

Success did not immediately roost on Mr. Brice's law sign. His "singular mental alertness" did not incline to the principles of the great profession he had chosen. He preferred the eccentricities of the practice, as applied to business affairs, in a manner that would bring quick returns and large dividends. For ten years the condition of Mr. Brice's law practice was such as to compel him to occupy a sitting position, in order to conceal the yawning chasm in the rear portion of his only pair of pantaloons. His labors at night, in the studious attempt to solve the fascinating mysteries of the great American game, draw poker, tended rather to aggravate the breach in the garment mentioned.

Mr. Brice has an equal and well balanced temperament, which is the greatest gift God and a good mother can give to a child born of woman. He is, or was, red headed, but amiable. The troubles that haunt such "mental alertness" as he possesses, have started the snow drifts in his abundance of hair. He is small of stature, and his presence is not commanding. An unusually large nose, and two blue eyes, set like sapphires out of place, in sunken craters garnished with ruby edges, present contradictions and a contrast that make the face a puzzle, and not always pleasing. His voice has a metallic ring, softened by a musical sound, that betokens a lack of sincerity. He talks out of one corner of his mouth, and seems to be holding the other three-fourths in reserve to surprise the market. You half feel, in talking to him, that like Joab, the captain of David's hosts, that in seductive tones he could say: "Hail, brother! How is it with thee?" and stab you under the fifth rib, if necessary.

Mr. Brice's nose is abnormally large, and with his deep set eyes, gives a vulture cast to his countenance. If it be true, as physiologists claim, that all great brains are accompanied with big noses, Mr. Brice's nasal adornment would indicate a large development of cerebral matter behind it, and thus account for his "mental alertness."

When Mr. Foster, along in the seventies, became interested in railroad enterprises, he had need of the services of an active and an unscrupulous lawyer, to secure rights of way, and to attend to other matters that called for business tact, rather than legal requirements, and fate led him to Calvin S. Brice.

This union, with a combination of returning prosperity and other fortunate circumstances, including Mr. Brice's "mental alertness," led to the formation of the famous Seney syndicate, in which Foster, Brice, Thomas, Seney and others, were the main springs, and originated a new industry. They became foot-pads and highwaymen along the great commercial ways in the land. Not the vulgar kind, that in days of old stopped the coach and robbed the passengers at the point of a yawning flint-lock pistol, but a new sort, fitting the new industrial conditions that had grown up.

Mr. Brice's "mental alertness," when brought in contact with the business methods of the great corporations and combinations, as the railroads and the Standard Oil Company, quickly grasped the manner in which the people were being robbed and squeezed. Mr. Brice's great brain, bold genius and audacity, devised the scheme for robbing the robbers and squeezing the squeezers.

Mr. Brice, in the contemplation of the industrial conditions, rightly concluded that there had been an unequal distribution of wealth. He saw the unlawful combinations defying the law, and enriching themselves by illegal gains stolen from the people. He resolved that he who could, by any means, take from these corporations a part of their wicked gains, would be a benefactor to his race, and a blessing to his age and country. Let every Buckeye, with heart overflowing with gratitude, be thankful that Ohio has produced Calvin S. Brice. The world has never seen his like, and the womb of time will never produce his equal. What Dick Turpin was to the highways of England in the last century, Calvin S. Brice has been to railroads of the United States in the nineteenth century. Mr. Brice made his first money in the Lake Eire and Western bunko game. He and his associates then began to carry out the scheme of milking the Hocking Valley and Toledo coal road, by building a parallel road to destroy its business and curtail its profits. M. M. Green, the president and father of this most successful road in Ohio, pointed out that there was only business enough for one road, and Mr. Brice then laid down his celebrated doctrine in the new commercial creed, "that railroads were built to mortgage or to parallel the prosperity of other roads." His share in the profits of the Ohio Central Railroad and Mining Companies, was said to be $100,000, and a wheel was then formed inside of the wheel, and a suit before Judge Jackson, in the United States Court, showed that a trust had been formed by which Mr. Brice's associates made contracts with themselves, by which the "tenderfeet" were beaten out of $3,000,000.

Mr. Brice kept under cover, but his "mental alertness" was rewarded by his share. The road went into the hands of a receiver. It was one of the merciful kindnesses of the Brice combine, when they had milked a property, to turn it over to the courts to recuperate. It is a fact, and may be only a coincidence, that every railroad property with which Mr. Brice has ever been identified, has become bankrupt and has been placed in the hands of a receiver, but Mr. Brice has always escaped from the wreck at an opportune time. Ohio had become too small for Mr. Brice's "mental alertness" and "capacity for affairs," and in 1880 he removed to New York City. He had acquired half a million in clear money in his two ventures in the Lake Erie and Western and Ohio Central. He looked about for new worlds to conquer. He selected the richest and most powerful railroad in the country as the subject for "paralleling," the New York Central Railroad. The Nickel Plate Railroad was devised. There was a meeting of the combine; one of them agreed to build the road from New York City to Buffalo, 512 miles, for $13,333,333.33. The Standard Oil magnates put up the bulk of the money. The road was built in a year. The attitude of the Standard Oil Company alarmed Mr. Vanderbilt. He did what Mr. Brice wanted and expected him to do. He bought the Nickel Plate Road for $26,530,000. The combine met in a Broadway office in New York City, to divide the spoils and rejoice. Mr. Samuel Thomas, who once carried off a blast furnace in Ohio when it was in operation, was so overcome by their success that he said: "My God, gentlemen, we are simply a lot of burglars. We might as well get a jimmy and dark lantern, and break into Mr. Vanderbilt's safe, and steal his money! It would be just as honest!" Mr. Thomas was right, but to break into Mr. Vanderbilt's safe, would require courage, and it would not be legal. In stealing, nowadays, we must comply with the forms of the law. Mr. Brice was so tickled with Mr. Thomas' playful remorse, that he taxed each one of the conspirators present $500, and purchased a badge for Mr. Thomas, representing, in gold, a broken safe with the door hanging by a hinge, burglars' implements lying around, and a diamond in the bull's-eye lantern. Only a mind in accord with the eternal verities, could conceive and execute the design of such an appropriate and poetical gift for a brother robber. Mr. Brice said he would put $500,000 in the nickel-plated unparalleled parallel, and he drew out $1,000,000 as his share.

Mr. Brice's audacity had "touched" the millionaires until he had become one himself. He was now a fixture in New York society and on Wall Street. He and his old partners became interested in the New York Aqueduct Works. In 1884, he swore he was a householder and resided in New York, and was worth over half million dollars, free from all debt and incumbrance. We cannot follow Mr. Brice in all of his dazzling and splendid career.

When oil and gas was discovered in Ohio, he and Mr. Foster became interested, and were stool pigeons for the Standard Oil Company, which tried to destroy the credit of the city of Toledo, and fought it for years in the courts and out, to prevent it from embarking in an enterprise of supplying its citizens

THE CAMPBELLS ARE COMING.

(*The Porcupine, Dec. 28, 1889.*)

with gas without being robbed by this monopoly. Mr. Brice had accumulated money enough to enable him to turn his attention to the world of politics, a field that would afford ample opportunity for exercising his "mental alertness" in its playful moods.

In 1876 and 1884 he was one of the electors on the Tilden and Cleveland tickets in Ohio. In 1888 he went to the Democratic national convention at St. Louis, Mo., in his private palace car, and took a number of poor and unsuspecting Ohio Democrats with him. This was a certain sign that he had designs of a political nature. His overpowering hospitality so overcame the Ohio brothers at St. Louis, that all sang his praises, and he was made the Ohio member of the National Democratic Committee, and then was chosen chairman of the Campaign Committee, after Mr. Barnum's death.

Mr. Cleveland was beaten, and the Democrats unexpectedly defeated, chiefly because of Mr. Brice's mismanagement. The Democratic Committee was annexed to Mr. Matt. Quay's organization. If Mr. Brice has the ability claimed for him, then he was a traitor to the cause of Democracy in this campaign. Mr. Cleveland was duly warned to beware of Mr. Brice's treachery four weeks before the election. After the election, Mr. Brice tried to cover up his foot-prints, in imitating Mr. Zach. Chandler in 1876, by telegraphing that Mr. Cleveland was certainly elected, when he knew he was certainly beaten, and he wanted him defeated. The result of this was that thousands of Democrats foolishly bet and lost their money on the strength of Mr. Brice's "electric" falsehoods.

VIII. By his prominence abroad, Mr. Brice had prepared the way for a purchase in Ohio. The Republicans, thanks to the misdeeds of Democrats during the Hoadly administration, had carried Ohio in 1885, '86, '87 and '88, four years in succession. The Republican Legislature (1889) had submitted three amendments to the Constitution to a vote of the people, namely: To remand the question of taxation to the Legislature; to elect members of the Legislature by single districts instead of by counties, and to abolish the annual elections. Experience has demonstrated that in Ohio it is always dangerous for a party to father changes to the Constitution, unless there is a well-founded reason for the changes, supported by a popular demand. There was no demand for these amendments to the Constitution. The Republican State Convention met in Columbus, June 25, 1889, and renominated Gov. J. B. Foraker for a fourth time and a third term. The committee on resolutions, composed of such men as Wm. McKinley and Gen. Chas. H. Grosvenor, who were opposed to Gov. Foraker and desired his defeat, failed to endorse or mention the amendments, because they were the pet children of Mr. Foraker's active brain. When called before the convention, Mr. Foraker in his speech of acceptance, with particular emphasis endorsed these amendments and did what the platform did not do: bound the party to their endorsement and made them an issue. In remodeling the election laws during the four years, the tendency had been in the wrong direction, of concentrating the power of appointing members of various municipal boards in the hands of the Governor. The people of Ohio, from the foundation of the State, as noted in the first chapters of this book, have viewed with apprehension the tendency to vest unusual duties and powers in the hands of the Governor. This fact, with the opposition to the amendments, and the prejudice against a third term, set the tide against the Republicans and placed their success in jeopardy, although intrenched behind the prestige of four consecutive victories. Our friend, Charles Foster, appears upon the scene again. It was understood that he was a candidate for United States Senator, and would furnish the money to conduct the Republican campaign. But Mr. Foster began to be crippled in his resources and could not produce as liberally as was his wont, and in addition he was notified that his friend, pupil and prodigy, Calvin S. Brice, was in the market to purchase the article, and Mr. Foster's zeal abated. Besides, he distrusted Mr. Foraker, and his attitude in the campaign was one of apathy, broken by an occasional speech. Mr. Foster's course in the Northwest, in connection with the disgraceful proceedings of the Standard Oil Company in his oppressing course in the gas fields, had aroused the people, and made them bitterly hostile to Mr. Foster, and it was not wise for him to be too conspicuous in the campaign, as he might jeopardize the success of the Republican ticket in close districts and counties. Although Mr. Payne still held his purchased seat in the Senate, the people had already forgotten the outrageous manner of his election, and in their forgetfulness were ready to make it possible to repeat the crime. The Democrats took advantage of the situation. Their State Convention met in Dayton, Aug. 26. The hopes of victory called together a large and enthusiastic representation of the party from all sections of the State. There were three pronounced candidates for Governor, Virgil P. Kleine, of Cleveland, Lawrence T. Neal, of Ross, and James C. Campbell, of Butler. Mr. Campbell was the only one that put any money into the canvass, but it was not enough to do more than organize his forces, and did not control the result. Mr. John H. Thomas, of Springfield, who was a candidate for Senator, cast his influence in favor of Mr. Neal, and spent some money to organize his forces. The first ballot resulted in Campbell getting 388, Neal 292, and Kleine 109. It required 395 votes to nominate, and on the second ballot Campbell received 399, Neal 299, and Kleine 93, and Mr. Campbell's nomination was proclaimed before the result of the ballot was announced, by the band playing "The Campbells are coming." The platform was a brief but vigorous arraignment of the Republican State administration, and a demand for home rule for both Ohio and Ireland.

The Republicans in their platform, in a state contest, had made a pathetic appeal for home rule for Ireland, and the Democrats thought it might be a good thing for Ohio. Mr. Campbell's speech of acceptance was in accord with the platform and indicated that the ground upon which the campaign would be fought, would be one of assault upon the weak points in the enemy's line.

Mr. James E. Neal, of Butler, a prominent and popular Democrat, and a former employee as an attorney of Mr. Brice's, was selected to manage the Democratic campaign. It was charged by the Republican press, that both Mr. Brice and Mr. John R. McLean were candidates for the United States Senate. This was prominently denied by both of them. Neither at this time thought there was any chance of Democratic success, and having nothing to lose, Mr. McLean had an understanding with Mr. Brice, that if the latter cared to enter the field, he would not be a candidate. Mr. Thomas was a candidate, and in response to the urgent request of Mr. James E. Neal, he made liberal donations of money to aid candidates for the Legislature in close counties. This money was sent through the Campaign Committee, and Mr. Thomas was allowed to amuse himself with the thought that he was on the road to promotion to the United States Senate.

The "silent and abhorrent forces" of the Standard Oil Company, stood grimly and patiently waiting in the background. If there was a chance of Democratic success, at the last moment, it would throw its gold into the scales on that side, and while it would never do to attempt to vindicate the father by another purchase of the seat, they could in a measure palliate the first offense, by "paralleling" it with a second in the election of Mr. Brice. If there was a probability of Republican success, their money and influence would go to Charles Foster, who had been so useful on many occasions.

Everything pointed to a Democratic victory, and at the last minute, Mr. Brice's agents stepped upon the scene, and just before the election the candidates for the Legislature were visited in all the close counties and sounded, and aided. In several instances, Mr. Thomas was astounded to have his money returned without explanation. Mr. Brice, with the aid of the Standard Oil Company, had "paralleled" Mr. Thomas' Senatorial line.

Mr. Brice put some $20,000 into the campaign before the election. It was only a drop in the bucket. The fight in Hamilton County was left to the direction of Mr. McLean and his friends, and the "golden grease" flowed in copious streams.

Mr. Campbell, as the representative of the honest,

earnest Democracy, was making the fight on principle, and up to three days before the election he despaired of success. He had no knowledge of the tremendous powers and money that were about to be turned loose to compel Democratic success.

There never was such adroit management on the part of the Standard Oil Company and their allies. Their campaign was managed from New York. They not only had to deceive the people, but the Democrats as well. They did both. With the valuable aid of Mr. Foster, they prevented the Payne scandal from becoming an issue in the campaign. The agents entrapped Mr. Foraker and Mr. Halstead of the Cincinnati *Commercial Gazette* with a ballot-box forgery, that proved disastrous to the Republicans. The parties that inspired the commission of this deed have never been exposed, and for some mysterious reason the perpetrator of the deed was permitted to drop out of sight, unpunished.

The election resulted in the defeat of Gov. Foraker by Mr. Campbell, by a vote of 379,423 to 360,561. The Prohibitionists polled 26,504 votes; the Labor party 1,048; and there were 195 scattering. The rest of the Democratic state ticket was beaten. Mr. E. L. Lampson, the Republican candidate for Lieut. Governor, on the face of the returns, had defeated Mr. M. V. Marquis by 23 votes. In a contest, Mr. Marquis was seated by the Senate, January 30, 1890. The Democrats had a majority in both branches of the Legislature. The following is a list of those elected, with their counties, the names of the Democrats being in italic.

The Senators were:

Thomas Q. Ashburn, Clermont; J. Park Alexander, Summit; *Perry M. Adams*, Seneca; *James Brown*, Hamilton; *John A. Buchanan*, Tuscarawas; *George F. Brady*, Huron; *Michael T. Corcoran*, Hamilton; Amos B. Cole, Scioto; Jeremiah L. Carpenter, Meigs; Henry J. Cleveland, Noble; *Daniel H. Gaumer*, Muskingum; Charles Herrman, Cuyahoga; George Hildebrand, Ashland; *Anthony Howells*, Stark; Winfield S. Kerr, Richland; *Virgil C. Lowry*, Hocking; *Henry C. Marshall*, Montgomery; David M. Massie, Ross; David Morison, Cuyahoga; Wilbur J. Nichols, Belmont; Jesse N. Orren, Clinton; James B. Pumphrey, Hardin; John K. Richards, Lawrence; *Andrew J. Robertson*, Shelby; Edmund A. Reed, Trumbull; *John Ryan*, Lucas; Geo. A. Schneider, Hamilton; *Joseph L. Stephens*, Warren; Thomas H. Silver, Columbiana; *John N. Soncrant*, Erie; *Melville D. Shaw*, Auglaize; *William W. Sutton*, Putnam; *Aaron R. Van Cleaf*, Pickaway; *William T. Wallace*, Franklin; Thomas B. Wilson, Madison; *John Zimmermann*, Wayne.

The members of the House were:

W. A. Blair, Adams; *Dewitt C. Cunningham*, Allen; *John D. Beaird*, Ashland; Leander C. Reeve, Ashtabula; William L. Kessinger, Athens; *Jacob Boesel*, Auglaize; Alexander T. McKelvy, Belmont; *William W. Pennell*, Brown; *Joseph J. McMacken*, Butler; *Thomas Goldrick*, Butler; Robert G. Kean, Carroll; Samuel M. Taylor,

Champaign; John F. McGrew. Clark; Douglas W. Rawlings, Clark; *Jonathan V. Christy*, Clermont; Wilford C. Hudson, Clinton; Alexander H. McCoy, Columbiana; *Jesse P. Forbes*, Coshocton; *Philip Schuler*, Crawford; Orlando J. Hodge. John P. Green. Wilbur Parker, J. Dwight Palmer, W. D. Pudney, Morris Porter, Cuyahoga; *Andrew C. Robeson*, *Harvey C. Garber*, Darke; Rollin K. Willis, Delaware; *John J. Molter*, Erie; *Thomas H. Dill*, Fairfield; H. M. Daugherty, Fayette; *John B. Lawlor*, *Lot L. Smith*, Franklin; Estell H. Rorick, Fulton; Jehu Eakins, Gallia; Elverton J. Clapp, Geauga and Lake; Andrew Jackson, Greene; David D. Taylor. Guernsey; *Frederick A. Lamping*, *Guy W. Mallon*, *William M. Day*, *Henry J. Schulte*, *James Nolan*, *Philip Dewald*, *John J. Rooney*, *Charles Jeffre*, *John J. O'Dowd*, Hamilton; Henry Brown, Hancock; *Michael F. Eggerman*, Hardin; Wesley B. Hearn, Harrison; *Dennis D. Donovan*, Henry; James M. Hughey, Highand; *William P. Price*, Hocking; *William S. Troyer*, Holmes; Lewis C. Laylin, Huron; Samuel Llewellyn Jackson; Charles W. Clancy, Jefferson; *Charles E. Critchfield*, Knox; George H. Holliday, Lawrence; Wilbur W. Wiseman, Lawrence; *Samuel L. Blue*, Licking; *Marvin M. Munson*, Licking; Charles M. Wanzer, Logan; William A. Braman, Lorain; James C. Messer, Lucas; Charles P. Griffin. Lucas; Joseph S. Martin, Madison; Lemuel C. Ohl. Mahoning; John R. Davis, Mahoning; *George B. Scofield*, Marion; Thomas Palmer. Medina; Joseph C. McElroy. Meigs; *Louis N. Wagner*, Mercer; John A. Sterrett. Miami; *Reuben P. Yoho*, Monroe;

Wickliffe Belville, Montgomery; *William A. Reiter*, Montgomery; Wm. B. Crew, Morgan; Wm. L. Phillips, Morrow; *Thomas J. McDermott*, Muskingum; *Chris. McKee*, Noble; *William E. Bense*, Ottawa; *Frank W. Knapp*, Paulding and Defiance; *Nial R. Hysell*, Perry; *Thaddeus E. Cromley*, Pickaway; *Almand Bayhan*, Pike; E. S. Woodworth, Portage; *Robert Williams*, Preble; *Milton E. McClure*, Putnam; *Charles N. Gaumer*, Richland; Elias Moore, Willis H. Wiggins, Ross; *James Hunt*, Sandusky; Joseph F. Coates, Scioto; *Alfred B. Brant*, Seneca; *Jachomyer C. Counts*, Shelby; *John E. Monnot*, Stark; *Edward E. Dresbach*, Stark; Henry C. Sanford, Summit; Thomas Wright, Summit; Charles H. Strock, Trumbull; *David L. Troendly*, *Elias R. Benfer*, Tuscarawas; John H. Shearer, Union; *Edward B. Gilliland*, Van Wert; *Stephen W. Monahan*, Vinton; Alexander Boxwell, Warren; Frederick J. Cutter, Washington; *Henry Roeser*, Washington; *Michael J. Carroll*, Wayne; *Charles A. Weiser*, Wayne; *Blair Hagerty*, Williams; George B. Spencer, Wood; *William C. Gear*, Wyandot.

There were 19 Democrats and 17 Republicans chosen to the Senate, and 61 Democrats and 53 Republicans elected to the House.

IX. As soon as the result was known, there was no longer reason for concealment. A few days after the election, in an interview in New York City, Mr. Jno. R. McLean announced officially that Mr. Brice would be the next Senator from Ohio.

The boisterous sounds of a jubilant Democracy rejoicing over a supposed victory of the people had not died away, before they discovered that they had been "bunkoed." Angry protests were made but they were futile. It was evident that the brutalities of the Payne infamy could not be repeated. The people were in no mood to be trifled with. Mr. Brice hurried from New York City to Ohio, to participate in the general rejoicing, and proclaim his candidacy for the Senate, but not his purpose to purchase it. Men were simply amazed at his impudence and audacity. He was not a resident of the state by his own oath, and had no claims of any kind upon the state or the Democratic party of Ohio. Had he dared to be as bold before the election as he was afterwards, Ohio would have given an emphatic Republican majority, as a protest against such rascality, as she has done every year since Mr. Brice has put the hand of the strangler upon the throat of Democracy, and should continue to do it until Briceism has been rebuked.

X. Mr. Brice took charge of his own canvass. His agents were sent on mysterious trips to counties that had elected Democratic members of the Legislature. Geo. W. Hull went to Ashland, Mr. Charles Lamison went to Monroe, Mr. S. S. Yoder went to Stark, Mr. A. D. Marsh went to Brown, and there was a "pernicious activity" in spots after these visits. The papers became profuse in Mr. Brice's praise, and the members elect became reticent and silent upon the Senatorial question.

The agents had done their work, and fixed their men, and there would be no payments made at Columbus, as was done by David R. Paige, in the Payne purchase. Mr. Thomas had his agents out, but they were only nibbling at the bait. He could not hold those he had helped, and who had solemnly given their promises before the election.

One of the papers, to endear Mr. Brice to the Democratic heart, told how, as captain of a company in the 180th O. V. I., had voted himself and all his men for Vallandingham in 1863. Mr. Brice was not of age, and as the 180th regiment was not in existence until a year later, the absurity of the story is apparent. Over $30,000 was spent on the press in four weeks, as pay for praise of Mr. Brice and to advocate his candidacy for the Senate.

The tactics to some extent resembled the methods pursued in the Payne rascality. If any one for any reason opposed the election of Mr. Brice, his character and standing was fiercely assailed. It was unpleasant to express a conviction or opinion in opposition. He was shrewdly desirous of bolstering his candidacy with as much respectability as he could command. When he thought a man could not be openly bribed, he was willing to promise some emolument or honor. He found out A. R. Van Cleaf could not be bought, and he offered him the receivership of a railroad, and received an answer which he has never made public. To confuse the situation and cover the tracks of himself and his agents, a number of candidates were bought out. When his residence was questioned, Gov. Hoadly made him out a resident of Ohio by telegraph.

The Legislature met and organized the first week in January, 1890, and the Senatorial caucus was held Thursday, January 9. To disarm suspicions and in deference to public opinion, an open vote was had, and the first ballot resulted as follows: Brice 29, Jno. A. McMahon of Dayton, 14; John H. Thomas of Springfield, 11; Chas. Baker of Cincinnati, 6; James E. Neal of Butler. 12, S. F. Hunt of Cincinnati, 2; John McSweeney of Wooster, 2; Geo. W. Geddes of Mansfield, 2; Geo. E. Seney of Tiffin, 2; Jos. H. Onthwaite of Columbus, 1. There were 79 Democrats, but 73 present, and it required 40 to nominate. On the second ballot, Brice got 53 votes, McMahon 13, Thomas 3, Seney 2, Baker 1, and Onthwaite 1. Mr. Hysell, who was elected Speaker because he was a workingman, and Mr. Brice, who wanted to show how beautiful it was for the sons of toil and the millionaire to lie down together in pleasant pastures, voted for Mr. Onthwaite. Messrs. Adams and Brant voted for Mr. Seney, Mr. Forbes of Coshocton, who had been sold out as a candidate for Speaker, voted for Mr. Baker. The three orphans who refused to sell and betray Mr. Thomas, were Messrs. Bayhan of Pike, Monnett of Stark, and Hagerty of Williams. Those who voted for Mc-

Mahon, were Messrs. Brady, Marshall, Robertson, Van Cleaf, Wallace, Belleville, Cromley, Donovan, McDermott, McKee, Mallon, Reiter and Scofield. Those who voted for Mr. Brice, were Ashburn, Buchanan, Brown, Cochran, Gaumer of Richland, Howells, Lowry, Ryan, Shaw, Soncrant, Stephens, Sutton, Zimmermann, Beaird, Benfer, Benz, Blue, Boesel, Carroll, Christy, Critchfield, Day, Cunningham, Dewald, Dill, Dresbach, Eggerman, Garbar, Gaumer of Zanesville, Gear, Gilliland, Goldrick, Hunt, Jeffre, Lamping, McClure, MacMaken, Motter, Monahan, Price, Pennell, Nolan, O'Dowd, Robinson, Roeser, Rooney, Shulte, Troyer, Troendly, Wagner, Weiser, Yoho. Mr. Brice was declared the nominee, and was sent for and made a speech, which he had carefully prepared, so certain was he that the purchase would be made. In this speech he dwelt on his love and devotion to tariff reform, and pledged himself to do all he could to bring about the accomplishment of this ideal of the Democratic mind.

On Jan. 15, in joint convention, the presiding officer declared that Mr. Brice had received 19 votes in the Senate, and Mr. Foster 14, and Mr. Brice had received 57 votes in the House, and Mr. Foster 52, and he declared the prodigy elected over his patron to the United States Senate. It was Boodler against Boodler, and the pupil had beaten his master. For a second time inside of six years, the Senatorship from Ohio, had sold to the highest and best bidder. Seventeen of the men who had taken Mr. Thomas' money, and promised to vote for him, kept it and voted for Mr. Brice. Nothing but Boodle could induce men to commit such perfidy. The instant the crime had been committed, Wm. P. Thompson and the Standard Oil crowd telegraphed their congratulations. They rejoiced because their rascality of 1884 had been vindicated by its duplication by Brice. The Hamilton County members did not get anything. Most of them were very sore and disappointed. Three or four of them were honest and not for sale. Mr. Brice presented each one of them with a photo of himself, nicely framed. One of them took the picture home, and removed it from the frame, expecting to find money in the back. He did not. He was very angry. Mr. Brice had votes enough without the Hamilton County delegation, and he concluded that it would be useless, if not dangerous to buy any of them. As usual, the members of the Legislature were left in a demoralized condition by the Brice canvass, and their appetite for money was aroused but not appeased. No attempt was made to carry out any of the pledges made by the party and candidates before the election. Bills were passed to authorize the Governor to appoint Boards in Cincinnati. They had elected a home rule Senator from New York, and Gov. Campbell, in violation of his pledges, proceeded to make appointments for Cincinnati. Had he had the courage to refuse to do that which was a violation of the platform upon which he was elected, it would have saved him some embarrassment and the party a great scandal, for before his term of office expired, he convened the Legislature in special session, to remove his own appointees in Cincinnati, for dishonesty.

XI. Mr. Brice took Mr. Payne's thoroughly boodleized seat in 1891. He took up the Standard Oil Company's work where Mr. Payne left it off. He favored the Mail Subsidy and all its jobs. Mr. Foster was in close touch as Secretary of the Treasury.

Mr. Cleveland returned to the Presidency in 1893. It took the Democratic party a year to carry out its pledges on the tariff. In the Senate, Mr. Brice combined with others to delay and defeat the tariff-bill. The sugar trust made $30,000,000 through his manipulation. This is all recent history. In August, 1894, Mr. Cleveland wrote letters denouncing Mr. Brice and others for their "party perfidy and dishonor." On August 27, 1894, in a letter to Representative Catchings, President Cleveland said:

"I take my place with the rank and file of the Democratic party who believe in tariff reform, and who know what it is: who refuse to accept the results embodied in this bill at the close of the war; who are not blinded to the fact that the livery of the Democratic tariff reform has been stolen and worn in the service of Republican protection, and who have *marked the places where the deadly blight of treason has blasted the counsels* of the brave in their hour of might. The trusts and combinations—the communism of pelf—whose machinations have prevented us from reaching the success we deserved, should not be forgotten or forgiven."

Mr. Brice was the chief traitor and manipulator in the most brazen performance that ever disgraced the Senate or betrayed a party. In the summer of 1894, at the Democratic State Convention held at Columbus, Mr. Brice being present and sitting on the stage, Mr. Clark, of Youngstown, on a motion in favor of making the candidate for Senatorship the nominee by convention to go before the people, said:

"Gentlemen of the convention:—What one of you looks to the United States Senate as the depository of the best intelligence, patriotism and statesmanship of this country? Not one.

"When any great public question is before the people for decision, who looks to the debates of the United States Senate for light?

"When a Senator is to be elected by a legislature, the question is no longer asked, what is his worth? Meaning, what are his talents, what his learning, what service has he rendered the state, or what service is he capable of rendering it? No, the question no longer is, what is *his* worth, but what is *he* worth? Meaning, how much money has he. As if in the conferring of honors, in this republic, the length of a man's head was to be measured by the length of his purse.

"No argument can make it clearer than the naked statement of these truths, that the Senate of the United States no longer commands either the confidence or respect of the people of this country. Every one of you know that it has become a mere rich man's club—it is the bulwark of special and corporate privilege, the nesting-place of understandings, combines and trusts. It was here that the hateful sugar trust lately raised its hydra-head, and in the name of the "Communism of pelf," seized the Democratic party by the throat and compelled it to stand and deliver. Over this whole question hangs the blazing, burning shame, that, under the present system, it is easier for a man of talent without fortune to find his way into the house of lords of England, than into the Senate of the United States.

"This is the bitter truth of the situation. Now for the remedy. It is furnished to our hands in the election of the United States Senators by the direct vote of the people, for which this minority report provides. We propose to you no novel experiment, but established Democratic doctrine and practice. It was tried in Illinois and the Democrats elected their first Senator since the war. It was voted on in California, and regardless of party lines, an almost unanimous vote declared in its favor. Two Democratic Houses of Congress have declared by large majorities in its favor, and the Democrats of thirteen states have declared it to be a Democratic policy. (A delegate cries, '13, unlucky number.') No! No! Remember it is the number of stripes upon our glorious flag, and the number is that of the noble colonies which established the sacred liberties which I plead with you to preserve.

"This is a question that rises far above men; it rises far above party; it is a question of your country. I plead with you, I adjure you to adopt this measure, not in the name of men, not in the name of party, but in the love of your country, and of plain, common, every day, old-fashioned honesty in politics."

XII. The events surrounding Mr. Brice's purchase of the Senatorship, finishes our personal contact with politics in Ohio. This knowledge, gleaned in an experience of nearly twenty years, is herewith submitted. We have not told all the truth, but we have given enough facts to answer the purpose of this book. The indictment is made. The accused are arraigned at bar. If the generation that has produced these men and methods, and suffered these evils, be too weak to try, condemn and punish the criminals, we take the case on appeal to the court of posterity. Let us hope that those who succeed us will have genius enough to formulate laws to stay this rising tide of evil, and courage and conscience enough to enforce them, and save our liberties and our institutions from the imminent perils which menace them.

It must be reform or revolution. Which?

It will come, in peace or by blood! The people will not be denied.

www.ingramcontent.com/pod-product-compliance
Lightning Source LLC
Chambersburg PA
CBHW020459270326
41926CB00008B/669
* 9 7 8 3 3 3 7 1 3 4 0 2 0 *